THE PASTRY CHEF'S APPRENTICE

This edition published in 2015 by
CRESTLINE
an imprint of Book Sales
a division of Quarto Publishing Group USA Inc.
142 West 36th Street, 4th Floor
New York, New York 10018

Printed by permission of and by arrangement with Quarry Books, a member of Quarto Publishing Group USA Inc.

First published in the United States of
America in 2011 by
Quarry Books, a member of
Quarto Publishing Group USA Inc.
100 Cummings Center
Suite 406-L
Beverly, Massachusetts 01915-6101
Telephone: (978) 282-9590
Fax: (978) 283-2742
www.quarrybooks.com
Visit www.Craftside.Typepad.com for a
behind-the-scenes peek at our crafty world!

10 9 8 7 6 5 4 3 2 1

ISBN-13: 978-0-7858-3256-0

Library of Congress Cataloging-in-
Publication Data available

Design: Paul Burgess: Burge Agency
Artwork: Peter Usher: Burge Agency
Cover Design: Paul Burgess: Burge Agency
Photography: All technique shots by
Kylee Hitz

Printed in China

AN INSIDER'S GUIDE
TO CREATING AND
BAKING SWEET
CONFECTIONS AND
PASTRIES, TAUGHT
BY THE MASTERS

THE PASTRY CHEF'S APPRENTICE
MITCH STAMM

CONTENTS

INTERVIEWS WITH THE MASTERS

WHO DOESN'T REMEMBER THEIR GRANDMOTHER'S SPECIAL CAKE, AUNT MIRIAM'S STRUDEL, A NEIGHBOR'S BROWNIES OR COOKIES, THE FUNNEL CAKE AT THE COUNTY FAIR, THE ÉCLAIRS AT THE CORNER BAKER, THE APPLE PIE AT THE DINER, OR A FAVORITE DESSERT IN THE SCHOOL CAFETERIA? THOSE MEMORIES STAY WITH US FOR LIFE, DELIGHTING AND HAUNTING US AT THE SAME TIME.

INTRODUCTION

Pastries punctuate the stories of our lives. They become reference points for special moments. We cherish those memories, and those treats become the gold standard by which all other pastries are compared. We chase those memories, returning to bakeries, fairs, and markets hoping to recapture those precious moments; we contact friends, neighbors, and cousins in an effort to dig up the recipes so we can relive those moments. Library and Internet searches provide clues that tease and taunt, yielding products that come close but never match the memory. The memories loom on the horizon; their elusive nature is strong enough to keep us searching for a lifetime.

My family had dessert every night after dinner. Except for some of my mother's baked goods, our nightly desserts were from the bakery. To this day, no evening meal feels complete without some sort of sweet treat at the end, whether it is the corner of a chocolate bar, half a cookie, or a fully plated creation.

HERO WORSHIP

Each of the pastry chefs profiled here was generous in sharing his or her time, knowledge, philosophy, and experience. They have sacrificed traditional work schedules and/or time with their families to provide pleasure and memories to people whom they will never meet. They go to work long before sunrise working on their feet all day.

They are historians, teachers, and mentors linking the past to the future. They nurture young, aspiring pastry chefs; they are involved in their communities and professional organizations.

Pastry chefs dedicate their lives to mastering a trade, a craft, and an art form, and along the way they give us extraordinary gifts. This story unfolds daily in large and small shops around the world. Quite often, the only praise or accolades many pastry chefs receive is second hand—many pastry chefs work hidden from view.

Croissants by William Leaman

Pastry chefs dedicate their lives to mastering a trade, a craft, and an art form, and along the way they give us extraordinary gifts.

BRINGING IT HOME

In a way, home baking enthusiasts are no different. They rise early, work in hot, cramped kitchens, scrub pots, wash countertops, purchase expensive ingredients, buy the latest cookbooks, and fret over the details with the same fervent obsession as the professionals. And they do it to bring pleasure, comfort, and joy to their family, friends, neighbors, and colleagues. It may not be possible for you to have a fully stocked professional kitchen, but it is possible to learn the properties and characteristics of ingredients and to understand the principles and techniques of production.

All chefs agree that the best place to start is with the fundamentals. Every pastry chef emphasizes the importance of knowing and understanding the core techniques that are used daily in professional kitchens. Pastry chefs do not memorize recipes; they understand how the formulas work. This enables them to elevate their pastries to a higher level and gives them the tools to be creative. In this book, we aspire to help you understand pastry making on a deeper level, to move beyond being just a recipe duplicator. Armed with the knowledge and guidance from professional pastry chefs, anyone with the desire and determination can create world-class pastries.

As in a professional kitchen, it is advised to read through the recipe before beginning. Organization of ingredients and equipment will facilitate production. Document your results using notes and photographs. Over time, your observations will be more acute, and corrective measures will flow from your knowledge. The pleasure you receive from baking and making pastry will increase with your understanding of the art and practice, practice, practice. It won't be long before you are sharing your knowledge and experience with your friends and family … and having a lot of fun in the meantime.

Passion-fruit mousse dome by William Leaman

Lady Fingers by William Leaman

TRANSFORMING A FEW BASIC INGREDIENTS INTO A VARIETY OF PASTRIES AS DIVERSE AS TENDER LADYFINGERS, LIGHT-YET-RICH CHOCOLATE MOUSSE, SOPHISTICATED TORTES, FRUIT TARTS, CREAMY ÉCLAIRS, AND CRISP BISCOTTI SEEMS MYSTERIOUS AND MAGICAL TO THE UNINITIATED. INDEED, PASTRY MAKING IS FREQUENTLY THE LAST FRONTIER FOR MANY HOME BAKERS AND ASPIRING PROFESSIONALS.

CHAPTER 1:
THE INGREDIENTS

Almost every pastry combines flour, butter, sugar, eggs, and salt. Frequently, other ingredients, including chocolate, nuts, spices, fruit, extracts, and especially vanilla, are added to enhance the basic flavors. An easy way to elevate your pastries is to use the most appropriate and the highest quality ingredients available for any particular process.

Familiarity with the properties and characteristics of ingredients used in pastry making allows pastry chefs to create classic pastries using traditional ingredients and techniques to achieve consistent results. An understanding of the ingredients affords pastry chefs the ability to create interpretations of the same traditional pastries. Re-interpreting and personalizing traditional pastries is one of the markers distinguishing pastry chefs from pastry cooks.

Speaking with the august group of pastry chefs featured in this book, I heard four recurring themes:
• Use the best ingredients.
• Respect the fundamentals.
• Document your results.
• Practice, practice, practice.

Of course, practice is the most fun part of this equation—more so when you are able to troubleshoot and solve problems. (However, it is even more fun to avoid them in the first place!) Ingredient selection and sourcing will become easier as you learn the manner in which they influence results. Then you'll be able to fix problems when they arise and manipulate recipes without compromising the integrity of the formulation. So let's start talking about the ingredients you'll use most often.

Protein numbers can be misleading. The quality of the protein is more important than the quantity.

FLOUR

Flour is the logical choice to begin the study of pastry ingredients, since it is found in all baked pastries. It is milled from wheat kernels to provide a variety of strengths, particle sizes, and other characteristics.

Pastries that include flour are typically leavened by physical, chemical, or biological means (more on this on page 15). Only wheat flour possesses the quality gluten-forming proteins necessary to trap these leavening agents. Flours from other grains—such as rice, corn, oats, rye, and buckwheat—contribute to the characteristics associated with regional and ethnic pastries; however, they are typically combined with wheat flour so that the pastries will have the gluten they need to be light, tender, and uniform.

Wheat kernels are seeds necessary for the perpetuation of the plant species. They contain the vital nutrients for the nascent stages of the next plant and are made up of three parts: the bran, the germ, and the endosperm. Bran is the protective outer coating, rich in minerals, cellulose, and fiber. The germ has an abundant supply of enzymes used to convert starches into simple sugars (useful for fermentation), fats, and vitamins. It is the embryo of the next plant. The endosperm is the largest part of the kernel and is made of starches, proteins, and carbohydrates.

There are other components in flour, such as fats and moisture; however, in pastry making, the main considerations are the quality and amount of starches and proteins. Starches absorb liquids and provide structure to baked goods. There are two gluten-forming proteins in wheat flour: glutenin and gliadin. Glutenin provides strength, elasticity, and gas-trapping properties to dough. Gliadin provides extensibility (the ability to stretch). Technically, there is no gluten in flour, only the gluten-forming proteins. When you add water to wheat flour and agitate or mix them, gluten is formed. When dough is properly developed, a web of gluten permits the dough to be shaped and expand during rising and/or baking (extensibility), yet controls the expansion and maintains the desired shape (elasticity).

CLASSES OF WHEAT

There are six classes of wheat among tens of thousands of varieties: *hard red winter, hard white winter, hard red spring, soft red winter, soft white*, and *durum*. These classes denote which part of the year the wheat is planted, the color of the grain, and the hardness of the grain. Soil conditions and climate affect the quality of the gluten-forming proteins.

Hard wheat left in the ground during winter absorbs abundant amounts of nitrogen, resulting in flour with high-quality proteins required for bread production. Too much moisture in the form of rain or snow dilutes the nitrogen content, and too little moisture creates a nitrogen deficit, adversely affecting the proteins.

Because of its pale color and shorter, more easily broken gluten, **soft white flour** works well for making cakes and pastries. Pastry flour is milled from **soft red winter** and/or soft white flour, and it is ideal for tart crust, cookies, pie dough and the like. Cake flour, milled from soft red wheat, is bleached white and is ground and sifted to a finer consistency than bread and pastry flours, which allows it to better absorb liquids and sugars. It is also softer than pastry flour, helping it impart the characteristic lightness and tenderness associated with cakes.

Durum has a substantial amount of protein; however, the balance of glutenin and gliadin is skewed, resulting in more extensibility and less elasticity, making it better for pasta than pastry. It is used to make bread, but in conjunction with other types of wheat flour.

Protein Levels in Flour

North American millers use protein content as a specification. European millers use the ash content of the flour, an indication of the mineral content. For example, in France, many bread bakers use Type 55 or Type 65 flour for bread making. That means that the ash content is 0.55 or 0.65 percent. The higher the number, the higher the ash content, indicating that less of the bran and germ (where the minerals are found) were discarded during milling.

ALL-PURPOSE FLOUR

A few words about all-purpose flour: It's good for everything and good for nothing. Pastry chefs use specific flours for specific purposes and products. With its wide range of specifications, all-purpose flour is best left on the market shelf. The specifications of all-purpose flour vary by geographic regions and tradition. For example, in the southern United States, all-purpose flour is very soft (low protein) for biscuits, corn bread, etc. There are many excellent regional and ethnic pastries that have been made with all-purpose flour for years; however, for predictable, consistent results, it is best to use specific flours for specific products. The resources available for the modern pantry thanks to specialty markets and the Internet have made formerly hard-to-find ingredients readily available. Disclaimer: If you have made a favorite recipe many times and used all-purpose flour, you should continue to do so. The recipes in this book were made with specific flours.

LOW-PROTEIN BREAD FLOUR

Low-protein bread flour manufactured for artisan breads typically has a protein level of 11 to 12 percent. Many pastry chefs use LPB in place of pastry flour when producing biscuits, scones, cookies, quick breads, and other chemically leavened baked goods.

Low-protein bread flour functions in a manner similar to that of an ideal all-purpose flour. It is strong enough for many tasks, including bread making, yet not too strong for tender cookies, biscuits, muffins, coffee cakes, Danish, and so on. You can use it for everything except cake and some tart/pie crusts. Pastry chefs and bakers prefer it because the specifications of the flour are more consistent from region to region, from season to season, and from year to year.

Occasionally, pastry chefs and bakers will dilute the protein content of stronger flour by exchanging a portion of bread or low-protein bread flour with pastry flour. Another method is to exchange a portion of the flour for cornstarch in some of the lightest cake batters, such as angel food or ladyfingers/roulade (see recipe page 113).

Protein numbers can be misleading. The quality of the protein is more important than the quantity. For example, preschoolers use drops of white glue to hold pieces of paper in place; carpenters use an industrial glue to hold their work together. But a gallon of the white glue would not hold something together that a few drops of the industrial glue would.

Looking at the chart to the right, you see that whole wheat flour has the most protein and think that if you used it in place of white flour, your products would have greater volume. The truth is, however, that baked goods made with whole wheat flour will have smaller volume because the bran flakes cut and shear the strands of gluten, impairing their ability to stretch.

PROTEIN CONTENT OF FLOURS

Whole wheat	14–15%
High gluten	14%
Durum	13%
Bread	11–12.5%
Pastry	8–10%
Cake	7–8.5%

SWEETENERS

Other than flour, sugars are the most commonly used ingredient in pastries. They contain carbon, hydrogen, and oxygen and are classified as carbohydrates. All sweeteners fall into two groups: monosaccharides and disaccharides. When using yeast as a leavening agent, monosaccharides are directly fermentable. Disaccharides must be converted to monosaccharides by enzymatic action in order to be metabolized by yeast.

Sugars come in many forms and from many sources. Pastry chefs usually select **granulated sugar** for creaming with plastic fats (butter, shortening, etc.) in the production of cakes, cookies, and similar products or for whipping with eggs (whether whole, yolks, or whites) in the production of cakes. Moist **brown sugars** are useful for bun fillings, cookies, cakes, and similar products. **Superfine sugar** is desirable for icings and high-ratio cakes (cakes that contain a higher ratio of sugar and liquid than typical cakes) made with the blending method. **Powdered, or confectioners', sugar** is used for flat (water) icings, stiffer cookies, tart crusts, and décor. **Honey, glucose, corn syrup, and agave syrup** are used for their distinctive flavors in specialty products, and they increase the shine of icings, frostings, and glazes. **Molasses**, a byproduct of sugar refining, imparts an unmistakable, earthy flavor and color to pastries, while **maple syrup** is prized for its subtle flavor.

FUNCTIONS OF SWEETENERS

Sweeteners play a wider role than just simply adding sweetness. Here are several other roles that sweeteners play in pastries. (Keep in mind, all sugars are not created equal. See the chart, "How Sweet It Is," to learn more about relative sweetness.)

Tenderizes: In solution (a dough or batter), sweeteners inhibit gluten development and starch gelatinization. Sugar is hygroscopic (it absorbs and retains moisture) and diverts a portion of the water from structure builders like gluten and starch, resulting in tender products.

Extends shelf life: This is also due to the hygroscopic properties of sweeteners. Honey, glucose, and invert syrups (made with equal amounts of fructose and glucose) keep products fresher longer than other sweeteners due to their increased hygroscopic properties. A hygroscopic ingredient attracts and retains moisture.

Promotes leavening: When you cream dry, crystalline sugar with plastic fats or whip it with eggs, the process traps air that is useful for leavening. (Read more about this in Chapter 3.)

Stabilizes egg foams: The dissolved sugar inhibits the unfolding and subsequent linking of the proteins. This is especially important when making meringues, whether for leavening baked goods or for aerating mousses. Superfine sugar works best for this application because it dissolves more quickly than other granulations.

Contributes to crust color and caramelized flavor: Sugar caramelizes when it is heated over 320°F (160°C). A caramelized crust is the first part of a baked good to touch the tongue, and it delivers a pronounced flavor. Some flavors from the crust migrate to the interior of the product, creating layers of flavor.

Complements: Sugars complement other ingredients, especially salt.

Contributes flavor: Sweetness is one of the five tastes. Sweeteners such as honey, molasses, piloncillo, palm sugar, jaggery, demerara, and muscovado imbue pastries with their unique, characteristic flavors.

Preserves: Sugars inhibit mold development.

HOW SWEET IT IS: A TABLE OF SWEETNESS VALUES

Sucrose, or table sugar, is considered the control in comparing the sweetness values of different sweeteners. It has a value of 100. For example, if molasses were exchanged with sucrose (by weight), because it has a sweetness value of only 70, the baked product would not be as sweet.

Fructose	172
Invert syrups	102
Sucrose (the control)	100
High fructose corn syrup	100
Brown sugar	97
Powdered sugar	97
Honey	80
Dextrose	75
Molasses	70
Maltose	65
Corn syrup (enzyme converted)	60
Malt syrup	42
Corn syrup (acid converted)	31
Lactose	16

A SPECIAL SWEETENER

Honey was the first sweetener harvested by humans. Cave drawings clearly detail the use of and value placed on honey. Different floral sources influence pronounced flavors in different honeys. Honey from a specific floral source is known as a varietal. Honey from multiple floral sources is referred to as wildflower. Honey is the only sweetener that does not require refining. When beekeepers harvest the honey, the activity in the hive has already refined it. Its benefits to baked goods are the same as other sweeteners, yet at a higher level. For example, honey contains amylase, an enzyme that converts starches to sugar, which is beneficial when included in yeasted breads. Its low pH makes it an ideal acid catalyst when using baking soda as a leavening agent (see page 15).

Honey is the only food that will not spoil. It may crystallize, however this can be remedied by immersing the container in hot water.

Some interesting facts about honey:

A bee weighs 0.004 ounce and can transport half its weight (0.002 ounce) in nectar.

For one pound of honey harvested, nine must be produced, with eight remaining in the hive to sustain the colony.

50,000 miles of flight time are required to gather enough nectar for those nine pounds, yielding one pound for human consumption.

The pH of honey is between 3.9 to 4.4, similar to sourdough bread.

Bees have two sets of wings, one to fly and one to fan nectar moisture out of the hive.

The internal temperature of the hive is 92 to 95°F (33.3 to 35°C), which reduces the water content until the honey consistency is achieved.

FATS AND OILS

If any food group other than carbohydrates has come under public (or media) scrutiny in recent history, it is most certainly fats. Fats and oils also consist of carbon, hydrogen, and oxygen. They are an important dietary source of body heat/energy. Fats are a mixture of triglycerides that are semi-solid or solid at room temperature. Oils are also a mixture of triglycerides; however, they are liquid at or below room temperature. Fats normally used in pastry kitchens include shortening, margarine, lard, butter, and oils.

Shortening may be of animal or vegetable origin, or a combination. It has a melting point of 110°F (43.3°C) and is excellent for creaming with crystalline sugars. Due to its high melting point, products made with it may leave a waxy coating in your mouth.

Margarine is made from partially hydrogenated soybean and palm oils and includes diglycerides and artificial flavors and colors. Professional pastry chefs largely eschew it. Its most notable benefit is its low cost. It is best left as a table spread.

Lard is rendered from the internal organs of hogs. It is the hardest of all fats. Like shortening, it is 100 percent fat. It is prized for its distinct smoky flavor in certain traditional pastries. Its hard, granular texture produces flakier pie crusts than other fats, and it is an excellent medium for frying. It has a melting point of 112°F (44.4°C). It is not as good for creaming.

All the recipes in this book call for unsalted European-style butter. American butter is 80 percent butterfat; European style is 82 percent. It is most pliable at 60 to 70°F (15.5° to 21.1°C). It is soft at 80°F (26.6°C), and it has a melting point of 88°F (31.1°C) with a final melting point of 94°F (34.4°C). It is the only fat that will melt in the mouth, creating a clean "finish" or luxurious mouthfeel. Butter flavorings have been developed in laboratories and added to other fats, but no other fat can match the complex flavor and mouthfeel of butter. European-style butter is especially beneficial for use in laminated dough such as puff pastry (see page 65).

Oils used in the pastry kitchen are derived from vegetable sources and have a greater tenderizing effect than many fats. Their flavor derives from their plant source. They do not contribute to leavening, but they produce a moister product with an extended shelf life. They are frequently used in quick bread products, such as *pain d'epices* (see page 40)

FUNCTIONS OF FATS AND OILS

Fats and oils, also known as lipids, are an essential food group. All fats and oils are derived from animal or plant sources. When choosing fat for a baked item, it is good to understand the source and the properties and characteristics associated with each type of fat. Some fats are better for creaming, others contribute to greater shelf life, or flakiness, or specific flavors.

• **Tenderizing:** Fat and oils encapsulate flour particles, rendering them impermeable to water. Gluten is less likely to form if water is unavailable to the flour. Fats coat gluten strands, lubricating and shortening them, making pastries more tender.
• **Flavor:** While shortening has no flavor, butter, lard, and vegetable oils have distinctive flavors.
• **Flakiness:** In pie dough, pieces of fat in the dough melt in the oven, creating layers. In puff pastry, layers of fat separate layers of dough. As the pastry bakes, the water in the dough leavens the product, and the fat keeps the layers from merging.
• **Leavening:** Air is incorporated into fats during the manufacturing process. Highly emulsified fats created for high-ratio cakes, such as shortenings formulated specifically for cakes and icings, contain up to 10 percent air. These and other fats trap additional air during the creaming process. Carbon dioxide and steam collect in the air cells created during creaming and allow the product to expand.
• **Body and texture:** Icings, frostings, and fillings benefit from the use of solid fats, most notably butter.

DEFLATING A MYTH

It is widely believed that the water in the fat used to laminate puff pastry is converted to steam during baking and that this steam leavens the pastry. Some of the flakiest puff pastry is made with special 100% shortening (0% water). In Europe, extra dry butter is used for lamination and has little to no water, yet the products made with it are quite flaky. Puff pastry dough is made with two parts flour and one part water. It is the water that leavens the pastry.

A LITTLE BIT ABOUT BUTTER

It takes 21 pounds (9.5 kg) of milk to make 1 pound of butter.

Unsalted butter is often referred to sweet butter; it should not be confused with sweet cream butter, which may or may not be salted. Most butter in the United States and Europe is made from sweet cream.

Cultured butter is made from fresh cream to which a lactic acid bacteria culture is added, resulting in a tangy, complex flavor.

The amount of salt in salted butter varies with manufacturers. Additionally, salted butter contains more water than unsalted butter. Using unsalted butter and adding a specified amount of salt to recipes will yield predictable, consistent results.

THE pH VALUE OF BAKED GOODS

The pH number represents the power of hydrogen to form ionic bonds. The pH level has a pronounced effect on baked goods, including their quality, flavor, and shelf life.

Low pH (Acid)	High pH (Alkaline)
Tart or sour taste	Soapy or sodalike taste
Whiter crumb	Darker crumb
Whiter crust	Darker crust
Reduced volume	Normal volume
Tighter grain	More open grain
Silky texture	Crumbly texture
Moister—longer shelf life	Moisture loss—shorter shelf life

LEAVENING AGENTS

Baked pastries are leavened by introducing one or more gasses into the dough or batter, creating products that are light and more easily chewed, are more digestible and palatable, and have greater volume. Leavening agents are categorized as physical, chemical, and biological.

PHYSICAL LEAVENING AGENTS

Air and steam leaven baked goods by physical means. Air is incorporated into mixtures by creaming plastic fats and crystalline sugar. The sharp edges of the sugar cut into the fat, trapping air in newly formed cells. It is in these cells that steam and/or carbon dioxide will collect and expand when heated. Products made with the creaming process include quick breads, cookies, and cakes. Another method of incorporating air is through the use of egg foams. Whipping whole egg, egg yolk, or egg white with crystalline sugar creates a stable foam of air cells that will expand when heated, as well as trapping gasses that will expand when heated. Products made by whipping eggs with crystalline sugar include ladyfingers, angel food cake, and genoise.

Steam is generated from the evaporation of moisture in certain doughs and batters. At 212°F (100°C), water converts to vapor and expands up to 1,600 times in volume. The rapid expansion leavens products such as pâte à choux (used to make cream puffs, éclairs, etc.) and puff pastry (palmiers, jalousies, etc.).

CHEMICAL LEAVENING AGENTS

There are two main chemical leavening agents: baking soda, also known as sodium bicarbonate, and baking powder. When you combine baking soda with moisture and an acid, it generates carbon dioxide. Baking soda has twice the gassing power of baking powder. It is alkaline, with a pH of 8.4 to 8.9, and when heated without an acid, it generates carbon dioxide and sodium carbonate, which combines with the fatty acids in the recipe to produce a soapy taste. Since baked products brown better when they're alkaline, baking soda promotes good crust and crumb color and may be used in conjunction with baking powder to adjust a recipe's alkalinity for this purpose. Baking soda also has a weakening effect on proteins. This contributes to spread in cookies, which contain proteins in eggs and flour.

The most widely used type of baking powder used by professionals and home bakers is double acting. Double-acting baking powder has a neutral pH of 7. Baked goods made with baking powder will generally have a pH of 6.5 to 7.5 (see chart above).

Double-acting baking powder is made from one slow-acting and one fast-acting acid ingredient, baking soda, and a filler starch to keep the baking soda and acids separated, preventing premature release of the carbon dioxide. It also absorbs moisture that may have been incorporated during manufacturing or from the environment. (Always keep baking powder tightly covered.) After mixing, 20 to 30 percent of the carbon dioxide is released at room temperature, leaving 70 to 80 percent to be released in the oven, giving it good "bench tolerance," or the ability to withstand the rigors of production and delays in production without any discernable damage. When exposed to heat in the oven, the generated gas seeps into air cells and is trapped by the coagulation of gluten and other proteins (such as egg white) in the recipe.

BIOLOGICAL LEAVENING AGENT

Yeast is used to leaven breads and pastries. In an environment of warmth, moisture, and an abundant food source, it produces carbon dioxide, which leavens baked goods. None of the pastries chosen for this book are leavened with yeast, so we will not spend a lot of time discussing it.

Understanding the composition of ingredients leads to a greater understanding of their contributions to the final product.

DAIRY PRODUCTS

All the recipes in this book that require milk were made with whole milk. Pastry chefs have many forms of dairy from which to choose: buttermilk, whipping cream, heavy cream, yogurt, sour cream, crème fraîche, and, of course, butter. They all originate with dairy cows. Some chefs use goat's milk to create different flavor profiles.

Their functions in baked goods are
• **Flavor:** Most dairy products are characterized as having a tangy flavor. Fermented dairy products (buttermilk, sour cream, crème fraîche, yogurt, and so on), have a more distinctively sour, or tangy, flavor.
• **Crust color:** Lactose, or milk sugar, is not fermentable by yeast, which means that when milk or milk sugars are used in yeasted dough, more sugars are available for crust coloration.
• **Nutritional value:** Dairy products contain protein, fat, sugar, and minerals. Incorporating dairy products in a recipe adds nutritional value.
• **Tenderizing:** The fat in dairy products, like other fats, inhibits gluten formation and lubricates gluten that is able to form.

Whole milk is an emulsion of tiny fat globules in a water solution of protein, sugar, and mineral salts. Its composition varies with the breed of cow, food available to the cow, time of day for milking, and geographic location. Fat and protein quality are the most susceptible to variation. Whole milk is preferred over skim and low-fat milks for pastry making due to its physical makeup. Products made with whole milk will have a more pronounced flavor, crust color, and nutritional value, and they will be more tender and have greater keeping qualities.

Most milk is pasteurized. Pasteurization is a process used to kill harmful bacteria. Unfortunately, all beneficial bacteria are also destroyed in the process. Milk is also homogenized, which prevents the separation of the fat and water. Milk is whiter as a result, and the flavor may be blander. There is a growing movement toward the consumption of raw milk. At this time, the only means to legally purchase raw milk is to purchase it at the site of production; it is not sold in stores.

Heavy cream is used as a liquid ingredient in baking products such as quiche, crème brûlée, and other custards. More often it is whipped and folded into mousses, Bavarian creams, and similar products. It may be sweetened and flavored as a stand-alone component, such as crème Chantilly (see opposite page). Heavy cream with a fat content of 40 percent is ideal for whipping. Most heavy cream available in the marketplace is 36 to 40 percent fat. When cream is whipped, air is incorporated. Fat globules link together and surround the air cells, creating a stable foam.

FERMENTED DAIRY PRODUCTS

Buttermilk, sour cream, yogurt, and crème fraîche are dairy products that have been acidified by the use of bacteria. Fermented dairy products are common in chemically leavened products such as scones, biscuits, muffins, and cakes, among others. Quite often the ingredient is used in the name of the product, such as sour cream coffee cake or buttermilk biscuits, due to the characteristics they impart to the product. The functions of these products in baked goods are:

• A distinctive tangy, and sometimes sour, flavor
• Increased shelf life by lowering the pH
• An increasing in the gassing power of products leavened with baking soda

A MILK SHAKE-DOWN
Understanding the composition of ingredients leads to a greater understanding of their contributions to the final product. For example, when using whole milk, the hydration is only 87 to 88 percent of an equal amount of water. If a pastry chef were using 100 units of milk in a recipe, he would be adding only 87 to 88 units of water, so a product might be drier than in a recipe that called for 100 units of water. This chart represents the components of standard whole milk purchased from dairies and markets.

Water	87–88%
Lactose	4.75%
Fat	3.65%
Protein	3.4%
Minerals	0.7%

WHIPPING CREAM

Some recipes advise adding sugar and flavoring before whipping cream. Another school of thought is that more air can be incorporated without interference from other ingredients. In either case, the bowl, whip, and cream should be very cold. For crème Chantilly, or sweetened whipped cream, use confectioners' sugar; with its 3 percent cornstarch, it "holds" the foam stable for a longer period of time. A typical ratio of sugar to cream is approximately 1 ounce (28.5 g) to 17.6 ounces (500 g). Measure the liquid by weight for consistent, accurate results.

To make crème Chantilly: Chill the bowl, whip, and cream. Whip at medium speed. When the cream is almost doubled in volume, add confectioners' sugar and flavoring, such as vanilla extract, if desired. Continue whipping to the desired consistency, a soft peak.

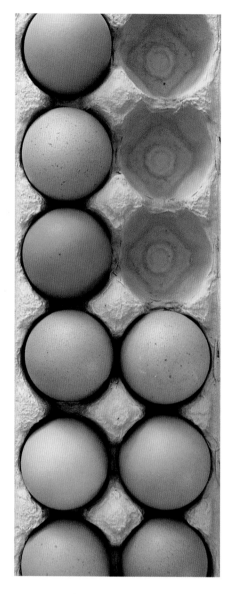

EGGS

An egg minus its shell is approximately 55 percent white and 45 percent yolk. In North America, large eggs average 1.76 ounces (50 g).

Functions of eggs in baked goods:
• **Tenderizing:** Egg yolks are approximately 50 percent moisture and 50 percent solids, which includes 33 percent fat. The fat in egg yolks functions the same as other fats in lubricating gluten strands and keeping gluten at a minimum.
• **Structure:** Albumen (egg white) protein and the small amount of protein found in the yolk coagulate when heated.
• **Leavening:** When eggs are whipped with crystalline sugar, air cells form.
• **Emulsification:** The lecithin found in egg yolks assists in emulsifying doughs, batters, and creams.
• **Nutritional value:** Eggs are a good source of protein and minerals.

• **Moisture:** Eggs are approximately 78 percent water (the remaining 22 percent is solids), which enhances keeping qualities.
• **Color, richness, and flavor:** Products made with whole eggs or egg yolks have a more golden interior, a more browned crust or shell, and, depending on how much egg is incorporated into the recipe, a distinctive "eggy" flavor.
• **Crust color:** Whole egg and water beaten together provide a golden shine when brushed on the surface of products prior to baking; whole egg, yolk, and water beaten together add a luster to the golden shine.

All recipes in this book use hen eggs. They should be as fresh as possible. Due to the high risk of salmonella, eggs should be handled with care. Inspect them before purchasing and do not use eggs with damaged shells. Store in a refrigerator and break eggs directly before using to prevent excessive decomposition. Wash your hands, equipment, and small wares after contact with raw eggs.

Eggs are most easily incorporated into other ingredients when they are at room temperature. It is best to remove eggs from the refrigerator one or two hours prior to use. Or you can remove them right before use and submerge them in warm water until they are at room temperature.

EGG COMPOSITION

Shell	Porous protective layer
Albumen (white)	87–88% water; 12–13% protein
Yolk	50% water; fat, lipoproteins, lecithin
Air cell*	Empty space at the wide end of the egg
Chalazae	Cord that keeps yolk suspended

*A small air cell indicates a fresher egg. Egg shells are porous; gas (oxygen) and moisture can pass through the shell. An egg loses moisture over time, and as moisture leaves the shell over time, the air cell gets larger.

FLAVORINGS

Scientists and chefs recognize four tastes: sweet, salty, sour, and bitter; and they dispute the existence of a fifth: umami. Yet we are able to discern thousands of flavors. It is estimated that flavor is 80 percent aroma and 20 percent taste. Orthonasal receptors alert us to the baking cinnamon rolls or apple pie next door or the orange being peeled behind us. They send signals to the brain as to the experience we can expect when consuming a certain product. Retronasal passages in the sinus and throat transmit the remainder of the information to the brain so that we may make distinctions between different foods, even those closely related, such as oranges, tangerines, tangelos, and clementines.

SALT

Salt, the organic compound of sodium and chlorine, is indispensible to life. A case could be made that it is equally indispensible in baking bread and pastry. It has a neutral pH of 7, permitting its use in almost all preparations. It harmonizes, enhances, and intensifies flavors. In yeasted dough, it regulates fermentation, tightens gluten, increases shelf life, and promotes crust color in addition to its flavoring properties. In pastries, salt assists in crust formation and color, it makes sweet taste sweeter and diminishes the impact of sour and bitter tastes, and it binds and strengthens the structure-providing proteins found in egg and flour.

Salt in formulations and recipes should be balanced. For example, for bread, you should use 1.8 to 2 percent salt in ratio to the weight of the flour. Other products include salt accordingly.

OTHER FLAVORINGS

Essential oils, extracts, emulsions, and compounds are available in natural and artificial forms. While natural flavorings may not be as uniform as artificial, they provide a truer flavor. They are less stable due to the evaporation and oxidization of some of the components.

Essential oils, also known as essences, are derived from fruits and plants and are highly volatile and aromatic. Stable oils such as clove and peppermint may be extracted by steam distillation. Fruits with soft rinds are hand-pressed to extract their compounds. Ether and alcohol solvents are used to extract other essential oils. Essential oils are more potent than extracts and should be used according the manufacturer's recommendations. Essential oils are more consistent throughout the seasons and the years than fresh fruit. Orange oil and lemon oil would be acceptable to use when recipes call for orange or lemon zest, such as *pain d'epices* (see page 41) or biscotti (see page 32).

Extracts are alcoholic solutions of flavoring compounds, such as vanilla extract. The flavor is typically between 2 to 8 percent essential oil. Extracts are available in natural and artificial forms and sometimes as a combination of the two. There are varying qualities of extracts on the market; purchase them from a reputable source.

Emulsions are widely used in commercial baking. They suspend volatile oils and aromatic substances in a water and glycerin solution or a water and gum solution. Pure emulsions contain 20 percent essential oil. They are stronger than extracts and are easily incorporated into batters. They are used primarily for baked products. Emulsions are a lower-cost alternative to essential oils. They result in recognizable flavors in the final product; however, they do not provide the clarity and brightness is obtained from extracts and essential oils.

Compounds, made with natural, artificial, or a combination of the two flavors, are available in fruit and other flavors. They are viscous solutions of flavorings and/or fruit pulp, sugar, and stabilizers used to flavor unbaked items such as Bavarian creams, pastry cream, whipped cream, mousses, and icings. Compounds are available in popular flavors such as mojito, tiramisu, piña colada, etc. Compounds make it possible to make several flavors of creamy fillings from one batch. For example, a pastry chef could make a single batch of buttercream and flavor one portion of it with Kirschwasser for the Black Forest torte, flavor another portion with mocha for another project, and yet another portion with another flavor of choice.

A VERY SPECIAL FLOWER

Vanilla beans are the pods of *vanilla planifolia*, the only edible member of the orchid family, which has over 25,000 varieties. It is indigenous to Mexico and is now harvested in many regions within 5 degrees of the equator. There are over 400 volatile flavor molecules in vanilla. By comparison, most red wines contain about two hundred. Vanillin, the major flavoring agent in vanilla, has been produced in flavor laboratories. Its flavor profile lacks the complexity and nuances of true vanilla. Using a vanilla flavoring that contains only vanillin will result in a monochromatic flavor profile compared to the sweet, floral, fruity, earthy, woodsy, subtle-yet-complex flavor of pure vanilla.

Milk Chocolate Truffles, Ewald Notter, page 145

CHOCOLATE

Linnaes, the great taxonomist, named the cacao tree *Theobroma cacao*; theobroma is Greek for "food of the gods." Chocolate is derived from this tree, which grows exclusively within the 20th parallel north and south of the equator. Ripe fruit is harvested and opened after a few days to separate the beans from the pulp. The beans and pulp are fermented at ambient temperature (tropical) to begin developing the flavor, and then dried. They are shipped and/or stored for cleaning, blending, and roasting, which encourages more flavor development. After roasting, winnowing removes the nibs, which are then ground, mixed, and kneaded and eventually conched, the final step in chocolate production. Conching improves the smoothness and "finish."

Chocolate has more than 600 volatile flavor molecules—remember, red wine has only around 200—making it one of the most complex flavors of all.

There are three varieties of cacao: Criollos, Forasteros, and Trinitarios. Criollo trees produce the highest quality beans. Because they are susceptible to a bevy of diseases, the yield is low—they account for less than 5 percent of all cacao harvested. Forestero trees, a hardier variety with milder flavored beans, account for most of cacao harvested and used. Trinitarios are hybrids of criollos and forasteros with characteristics of both.

Dark chocolate is made of cacao solids, cocoa butter, and sugar. The amounts of sugar vary, accounting for bitter, semisweet, bittersweet, and sweet chocolates. They are advertised as a percentage, such as 60 percent chocolate, which indicates 60 percent cacao solids and cocoa butter (meaning there is close to 40 percent sugar in the chocolate). The greater the percentage, the stronger the chocolate flavor. Milk chocolate is made of a reduced amount of cacao solids and cocoa butter. The higher percentage of sugar and milk solids can overwhelm the chocolate flavor.

Manufactured chocolate is categorized by its purpose:
• Industrial chocolate (mass marketed) is made from the lowest-quality beans and has the lowest amount of cacao solids and cocoa butter. It usually contains large amounts of sugar and milk or milk solids. Sweetness is the dominant flavor. It is not recommended for baking and pastry.

• Gourmet chocolate (high-end specialty) is made from select beans, either a blend or single origin. It benefits from using more cacao solids and cocoa butter. The flavor and finish of the chocolate is pronounced, smooth, and lingering.
• Couverature (finishing product) contains a minimum of 32 percent fat, which, prior to the year 2000, came exclusively from cocoa butter. Currently, other fats are permissible; however, reputable chocolate manufacturers have disregarded the concessions made to candy manufacturers and have remained true to their original mission of providing the highest quality products made with cocoa butter. Couverature, when tempered, provides shine, finish, snap, flavor, and other qualities to enrobed candies and pastries. With its higher percentage of cocoa butter, couverature is more fluid when melted, resulting in improved shine and snap when used for dipping, enrobing, or molding chocolate confections. It is available in white, milk, and dark forms. See Resources, page 172.

COCOA POWDER

After the cacao beans are roasted and the nibs have been separated, the nibs are ground to a paste. The grinding process creates heat, which liquefies and releases most of the cocoa butter. The remaining mixture is referred to as chocolate liquor. When chocolate liquor is cool, it is firm and known as unsweetened chocolate. Cocoa is the powdered version of chocolate liquor. It is used to flavor and color pastries.

Natural cocoa has a slightly low pH between 5 and 6, making it useful for increasing the gassing power of baking soda. Dutched, or dutch-processed, cocoa has been treated with an alkali to neutralize its acidity, raising its pH to 7 or higher. This darkens and casts a reddish tint to the cocoa in addition to softening and mellowing the bitterness of natural cocoa.

SPICES

Spices are aromatic plant products used to uniquely season pastries and savory foods. Volatile oils provide their characteristic flavors and aromas. They are classified according to the part of the plant used.

PLANT PARTS AND TYPES OF SPICES

This chart lists several plant parts and examples of spices that come from those plant parts.

Root	Ginger
Bud	Clove, Lavender
Bark	Cinnamon
Fruit	Allspice, Star Anise
Seed	Sesame, Poppy, Caraway, Cardamom, Nutmeg, Anise

CINNAMON: BARK & BITE
Cinnamon is from the dried inner bark of the Asian cinnamon tree. Quality (volatile oil content) is determined by the position of the bark in relation to sunlight. Trees or parts of trees that are shaded produce the highest quality oil. It's possible for one side of a tree to yield a higher quality bark than the other side.

The main classifications of cinnamon are Ceylonese (or Sri Lankan) and cassia. Sri Lankan, with its subtle flavor and light tan color, is considered by many to be the highest quality. Cassia, which is redder, stronger, and "hotter," is more widely used.

HERBS

Herbs, which were once used only in cooking, have been growing in popularity with pastry chefs, who are using them in both sweet and savory pastries. Dried herbs will be more consistent in flavor; however, fresh will always provide a truer, more complex flavor. Rosemary, thyme, tarragon, basil, and other leafy green plants have passed members of the mint family in usage in the pastry kitchen. Paired with more traditional pastry ingredients, they add floral accents and inflections. Rosemary/apple, sweet basil/melon, lemon thyme/strawberry are examples of combinations that work well together. Most herbs were originally used for medicinal purposes—much of their early use was based on folklore and superstition. Some were believed to cause illness and bad luck. Other herbs were believed to encourage good health and good fortune, in addition to warding off evil. Beginning in the thirteenth century, herbs became more mainstream as a flavoring agent in the kitchen.

EVERY PASTRY CHEF'S KITCHEN SHOULD BE WELL STOCKED WITH SPECIALIZED ITEMS AND TOOLS. PURCHASING THE ITEMS IN THIS SECTION DOES NOT GUARANTEE PASTRY PERFECTION, HOWEVER; THE RECIPES IN THIS BOOK DEPEND ON ACCURACY AND PRECISION.

CHAPTER 2:
EQUIPMENT AND TECHNIQUES

Many of these items can be used for other projects in the kitchen. Tools that are used for precise measurements are more important than flashy tools or tools that make jobs easier; begin building your toolkit with these items.

Digital scale with metric and U.S. imperial readings. Weighing ingredients is more accurate and efficient than volumetric measuring. The metric system allows for even greater precision than working with the U.S. Imperial system. Digital scales are inexpensive, small, and easy to use. Look for one that measures up to 11 pounds (5 kg) in increments of 1 gram.

Subgram digital scale with measurements to 0.1 gram. This is useful for accurately weighing minute amounts of ingredients. A variance of one or two grams of flour might not adversely affect the results of most recipes, but a similar difference in chemical leavening or salt could create a less-than-desirable product. These scales are more accurate for smaller weights. If you do not wish to purchase a sub-gram scale, an alternative method of measuring would be to use one of the digital scales mentioned above, but do not tare after the preceding ingredient. For example, if you weigh 500 grams of flour and need 2 grams of baking powder, do not tare the scale after measuring the flour and add the baking powder until the reading is 502 grams.

Graduated measuring cups and spoons. Measuring cups and spoons may be used for liquids or if you opt not to weigh your dry ingredients. The recipes in this book were measured by scooping and scraping the tops of the cups and spoons with a flat edge. When sifting was required, it was done after measuring.

Stand mixer with whip, paddle, and dough hook attachments. A stand mixer saves time, energy, and creates consistent products.

Digital thermometer. They read quickly and accurately. Some come with alarms that can be set to a desired temperature, and some have timers. These are useful for determining the temperature of cooked solutions such as the syrup for pâte à bombe or Italian meringue, tempering chocolate, or checking the doneness of baked goods.

Oven thermometer. Even if your oven is calibrated periodically, an oven thermometer will allow you to bake in the same conditions every time.

Commercial-weight aluminum baking pans with rolled edges conduct heat evenly. They are referred to as half sheet pans.

Nonstick parchment paper

Set of graduated mixing bowls

An 8-inch (20 cm) chef's knife, a paring knife, and a serrated slicing knife

Micro zester. This is useful for removing the zest of citrus fruits. It leaves the bitter pith behind, extracting only the zest with its essential oils.

Fine screen sifter. Useful for sifting ingredients or dusting finished items with confectioners' sugar.

Heavy-bottomed pots. Purchase at least one large 5- to 6-quart (5 to 6 L) pot and one smaller pot.

Wire whisks (two): A heavy, stiff one for items like pastry cream, and a thin one for whipping foams like heavy cream or egg whites.

Silicone baking mats. Baking parchment is useful and practical, but these nonstick mats are completely reusable.

Rounded bowl scrapers

Stiff, heatproof spatulas for folding and stirring

Flat-bottomed heat-proof spoons for cooking pâte à choux, caramelizing sugar, and stirring any thick mixtures

Disposable pastry bags. They are not very "green," but they are more sanitary than the reusable type. They may be used many times if they are washed between uses.

An assortment of pastry tips. You'll use these for decorating and producing items such as éclairs (see page 56), ladyfingers (see page 113), meringue, (see page 169), madeleines (see page 133), etc.

Icing spatulas. Choose one straight spatula for finishing cakes (such as the Black Forest torte on page 125) and one offset spatula for spreading batters (such as ladyfingers, see page 113). Both are used for many other functions as well, such as lifting a tart, moving components, etc.

Dough cutter or bench scraper

(Optional but useful) A torch is useful for heating a mixer bowl of cold ingredients, caramelizing crème brûlée, or loosening items from their baking vessels.

THE INGREDIENTS IN MOST PASTRY RECIPES ARE SIMILAR, IF NOT THE SAME. SO HOW IS IT POSSIBLE TO CREATE SO MANY DIFFERENT STYLES OF PASTRIES? OF COURSE, DIFFERENT PROPORTIONS OF INGREDIENTS ARE RESPONSIBLE FOR SOME OF THE DIFFERENCES. BUT THE REAL DIFFERENCE IS FOUND IN HANDLING, OR THE TECHNIQUES. HERE IS AN OVERVIEW OF COMMON, TRADITIONAL PROCESSES USED TO MAKE PASTRIES.

DOUGHS AND BATTERS

The **creaming process** is used for cookies, quick breads, and cakes. It requires crystalline sugar and a plastic fat (butter, shortening, or margarine). For successful results, follow the guidelines listed below.

1 Work with all ingredients at room temperature.

2 Cream the plastic fat with crystalline sugar until pale yellow and light. The sharp edges of the sugar cut into the fat, creating air cells that become a place for gasses (carbon dioxide and steam) to collect and expand when heated, leavening the product.

3 Add the eggs gradually to ensure a stable emulsion. If the eggs are added too quickly, the emulsion may curdle.

4 Using a curved plastic bowl scraper, scrape the bowl and mixer paddle to free any clumps of fat and/or sugar.

5 Add the blended dry ingredients; mix on low speed just until the mixture is homogenous. Overmixing results in the product imperfections of tunneling, toughness, and irregular shapes.

The **rubbing** or **biscuit method** coats the particles of flour with fat, encapsulating them. The liquid in the recipe cannot penetrate that barrier and is less likely to combine with the flour to form gluten, resulting in a more tender product. Keep the following principles in mind when using the rubbing/biscuit method.

1 Cube butter or other plastic fat and refrigerate.

2 Sift together the dry ingredients.

3 Using a stand mixer with the paddle attachment, or a scraper if mixing by hand, cut or rub the fat and flour mixture until it is the desired consistency. (For flaky crust, some particles of fat are left intact; for a tender crust or product, the fat and flour mixture are rubbed to a sandy consistency with no remaining lumps of fat.)

4 Add the liquid ingredients all at once and combine.

5 Mix until just combined.

The **blending** method is typically used when liquid fats are part of the recipe or when the recipe includes a large amount of liquid ingredients and no fat, as with *pain d'epices* (see page 41).

1 Combine all liquid ingredients and blend thoroughly.

2 Combine all dry ingredients and blend to evenly distribute the leavening agent, salt, and any other dry ingredients.

3 Add the dry ingredients to the liquid ingredients.

4 Mix just until incorporated.

FOAMS

Foams are used to lighten and/or leaven mixtures. Foams are made by whipping air into egg white, whole egg, egg yolk, or any combination of the above. Crème Chantilly is also considered a foam; however, it is not used to leaven. It is frequently used to lighten mixtures such as chocolate mousse (see page 89).

Whipping egg whites requires the most care of all foams. To create a stable foam of egg whites, first clean the bowl with hot, soapy water. Rubbing the bowl with a cut lemon and wiping with a paper towel to cut any remaining grease will lower the pH of the bowl surface. Egg whites are alkaline, so adding an acid can strengthen the foam, which is why many recipes call for the addition of cream of tartar when whipping egg whites. Begin whipping on medium speed to uncoil the proteins so they can begin linking together. Continue mixing on medium speed while adding sugar gradually. Continue mixing until the foam is stable. Whipping on high speed deflates the foam as quickly as air is introduced, and the foam can become overextended, making it less shiny and giving it a grainy texture.

When whipping whole egg or whole egg and yolk, the foam should reach the "ribbon stage." When whipped properly, air is trapped in the foam, which thickens it to the state that the foam collects or "ribbons" on top of the foam when you drop a small amount back onto the surface. When the foam achieves the ribbon stage, it has enough air available for leavening.

Stiff, whipped egg whites

COOKED PREPARATIONS

Each of these preparations takes place on the stove to provide the intrinsic characteristics identified with the products in which they are used.

Pâte à bombe, also called bombe paste, is used to stabilize and provide the proper thickening and texture to mousses and other creams. It is a mixture of whipped egg yolk and sugar syrup that has been cooked to 250°F (121°C). The syrup may be made from sugar and water; glucose and water; or sugar, glucose, and water.

Italian meringue is used to stabilize egg whites for use in macarons, buttercreams, and other pastries. It can also be used to lighten mousses. It is a mixture of whipped egg white and sugar syrup that, like the syrup in pâte à bombe, has been cooked to 250°F (121°C).

Pâte à choux has characteristics of both dough and batter. Flour is added to a mixture of boiling water and fat. This gelatinizes the starch and tenderizes the gluten, permitting voluminous expansion that creates a hollow container with a crisp shell that can hold sweet and savory fillings without damage due to moisture.

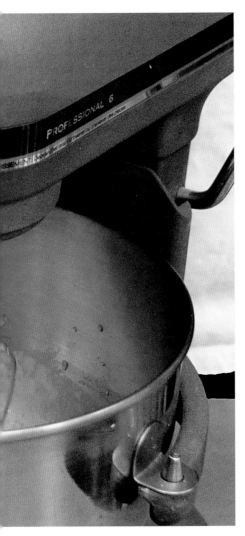

A sturdy stand mixer is necessary for whipping, blending, creaming, and kneading.

TEMPERING CHOCOLATE

Cocoa butter crystals are destabilized when chocolate is melted for coating candies and pastries. Tempering is the restabilizing of these crystals so the final product will have a thin coating that is smooth, shiny, and has a clean snap. There are several methods of tempering, such as tabling or seeding (vaccination method), during which the chocolate is melted, cooled, and in some cases, heated again. These are traditional methods with great merit and value.

A simpler and increasingly popular method with professionals and home bakers, is the direct method. To temper chocolate using the direct method:

• Use an accurate thermometer and a rubber spatula.
• Place the chocolate in a nonreactive bowl and microwave on a medium setting. Depending on the amount, microwave for 20 to 30 seconds, remove the bowl, stir, and repeat. Continue microwaving in 10-second intervals, stirring in between.
• Monitor the temperature to ensure that the chocolate does not exceed 90°F (30.2°C).
• When all the chocolate is melted, but before the temperature has reached 90°F (30.2°C), evaluate the chocolate to assure that it is "in temper." If some of the chocolate is still solid, return the bowl to the microwave for a few seconds, increasing the temperature to 91°F (32.7°C). Stir until melted. This process may be repeated, increasing the temperature to a maximum of 94°F (34.4°C). Do not exceed 94°F (34.4°C) or the chocolate will be unusable.
• Use for molding, enrobing, décor, etc., monitoring the temperature and adjusting as necessary.
• To maintain the temper, set the bowl over a pot of 90°F (30.2°C) water or occasionally microwave the chocolate for 10 seconds. A heating pad covered with a towel also works well to maintain the temperature. The chocolate should remain warm and fluid.

OTHER TECHNIQUES

Folding whipped cream or egg white into a batter or cream determines the lightness of the product. Aggressive or excessive folding can deflate the foam that is being folded into the other ingredients. Successful folding is easy but should not be taken for granted. These guidelines will help you understand this simple, but often misunderstood, technique.

• Use a flexible yet firm spatula.
• Holding the spatula vertically, begin in the twelve o'clock position and draw a straight perpendicular line to the six o'clock position.
• Rotate the spatula 45 degrees and move the edge of the scraper to clean the side of the bowl as you move toward the nine o'clock position.
• Lift the scraper and fold the mixture over on itself in the center of the bowl.
• Rotate the bowl 90 degrees and repeat the folding motion.
• Repeat until the mixtures is homogenous and lightened.

"*Creating new products and menus requires more thought, study, and time than people would imagine.*"

CHEF KANJIRO'S MODESTY AND HUMILITY CONCEAL HIS FIERCE COMPETITIVE NATURE. HE LIVES AND WORKS TO BE BETTER—NOT TO BE BETTER THAN OTHERS, BUT TO BECOME BETTER EVERY DAY. WHAT IS GOOD TODAY MAY NOT BE AS GOOD TOMORROW. THIS PHILOSOPHY HAS GUIDED HIM IN HIS LIFE AND HIS CAREER.

KANJIRO MOCHIZUKI,
EXECUTIVE PASTRY CHEF AT THE
IMPERIAL HOTEL IN TOKYO

INTERVIEW WITH KANJIRO MOCHIZUKI

IN SUCH A TRADITIONAL CULTURE, HOW DOES THE JAPANESE PUBLIC PERCEIVE THE CAREER OF PASTRY CHEF?

Japanese people love tea time, with not only green tea and sweet red bean types of pastries, but also delicious Western-style pastries. So pastry chefs are quite appreciated and famous, like iron chefs in Japan.

WHAT TYPE OF TRAINING DID YOU RECEIVE IN THE BEGINNING?

HOW HAS TECHNOLOGY CHANGED PASTRY MAKING?

Basic things have not changed so much. New tools such as flexipans and vacuum sealers, and new ingredients such as inverted sugar and agar-agar, have created possibilities for creating new products.

WHAT HAS BEEN THE MOST CHALLENGING AND/OR REWARDING JOB YOU HAVE HAD?

Two memories stand out. One was a large

WHAT IS YOUR THOUGHT PROCESS WHEN CREATING A DESSERT MENU?

When I discover new ingredients or have a new idea to use tools or ingredients, I am motivated to create new pastries and desserts. I place the guest's preferences before my own tastes. Naturally, the season influences menu construction, and lastly, I pay attention to trends. We ignore fads, but pay attention to trends. In addition, I must consider the concept of the restaurant and/ or banquet.

OTHER THAN BUTTER, FLOUR, SUGAR, EGGS, AND SALT, WHAT ARE THE FIRST TEN INGREDIENTS YOU WOULD SELECT FOR YOUR KITCHEN?

Seasonal fruits, chocolate, nuts, heavy cream, spices, gelatin, cheese, tea, liquor, and milk.

OTHER THAN AN OVEN, WHICH ITEMS ARE ESSENTIAL TO EQUIP

Dorayaki is a Japanese confection made from kasutera and a filling of sweet red bean paste. It is reflective of the pastry types created by Chef Kanjiro.

WHAT WAS THE MOST DIFFICULT SKILL FOR YOU WHEN YOU WERE BEGINNING YOUR CAREER?

We cooked 30 kg [13.6 lb] of pastry cream by hand every day, and the youngest one was in charge of it. I seemed to remain the youngest one for a long time. To cook that amount of it without scorching was almost impossible for me at that time! Now, I can cook any size batch of pastry cream without giving it a second thought. I'm glad I never gave up.

WHAT DO YOU BAKE AT HOME?

I only make cakes for birthdays at home, especially for my daughter.

WHAT TYPES OF PASTRIES/DESSERTS ARE MADE IN THE TYPICAL JAPANESE HOME?

Pan cakes and custard pudding are very popular to make at home.

WHAT IS YOUR GREATEST STRENGTH? WHAT IS YOUR BIGGEST WEAKNESS?

My strength: Selecting the people who work with me—recruiting, training, and bringing out their best abilities. My biggest weakness: I cannot say no! Especially when somebody asks me to play golf.

HOW DO YOU STAY MOTIVATED?

I love my job, I love my profession, and I love the people I work with. So I stay automatically motivated.

WHAT ARE YOUR GOALS FOR THE FUTURE?

I do not aim at one particular thing right now, but my dream is to educate, coach, and train other chefs for international pastry competitions.

WHAT ARE YOUR WORDS TO LIVE BY?

Do your best and think before complaining.

BISCOTTI
BY KANJIRO MOCHIZUKI

Biscotti, or twice-baked cookies, have become a fixture of coffee shops and cafés over the last few decades. Originally, they were baked twice as a means of preserving them. Toasting, the second bake, imparts lingering toasty, malted notes, highlighting the natural flavors of the other ingredients. Some retailers keep them on display until they are sold out, citing the "they are supposed to be hard and dry" page of their training manual. Eating biscotti after they have been freshly baked (as opposed to sitting in jars for months) will rejuvenate anyone's appreciation for them. They will remain fresh in an airtight container for one week.

INGREDIENTS

	U.S. Imperial Weight	Metric Weight	Volume
Unsalted butter*	8 oz	227 g	1 cup
Granulated sugar	12 oz	340 g	1½ cups + 3 tablespoons
Orange zest			From half an orange
Whole egg			5 eggs
Vanilla extract			1 tablespoon + 1½ teaspoons
Flour	1 lb, 8 oz	680 g	5 ⅓ cups
Baking powder	1.8 oz	50 g	⅓ cup + 2 tablespoons
Salt	0.5 oz	14 g	2 teaspoons
Cinnamon	0.06 oz	1.7 g	¾ teaspoon
Walnuts, toasted and coarsely ground or chopped*	12 oz	340 g	3 cups unchopped chopped
Tempered couverture for dipping (optional, page 27)			

Recipe notes: *Use European-style butter (minimum 82% fat content).
**Any nut may be substituted.

The biscotti may be frozen directly after slicing and toasted as needed.

Make large biscotti by dividing the dough into 1 pound, 15 ounce (824 g) pieces, and then rolling into 24-inch (61 cm) logs. Proceed as directed above.

Adding zest to the butter and sugar during the creaming stage helps extract more of the orange flavor. In addition to creating air cells in the butter, the crystalline edges of the sugar cut into the zest, releasing more of its essential oils. And, the zest will be more evenly distributed.

PROCEDURE (see photos, page 34–35)

1 Preheat oven to 350°F (180°C or gas mark 4).

2 In the bowl of a stand mixer fitted with a paddle attachment, cream the butter, sugar, and orange zest on medium speed until pale yellow, lightened, and well mixed (a).

3 Combine the eggs and vanilla. Add the mixture gradually to the creamed butter mixture (b) while mixing on medium speed. Add the eggs in several increments, waiting for each addition to incorporate before adding the next (this helps to create a stable emulsion).

4 Turn off the mixer. Using a plastic bowl scraper, scrape the sides of the bowl and paddle.

5 In a medium bowl, blend the flour, baking powder, salt, and cinnamon. Add to the butter/egg mixture.

6 Mix lightly on low speed until just combined.

7 Add the walnuts (c) and mix on low speed until smooth.

8 Divide the mixture into 14.5-ounce (412 g) portions (d).

9 Form into logs and roll to almost the length of a half sheet pan, approximately 12 inches (30 cm) (e, f).

10 Place the logs on a sheet pan lined with parchment paper.

11 Press the top of the logs lightly to flatten the tops (g). The height should remain the same; you're just minimizing the curve.

12 Place on the middle shelf of the oven and bake until the logs are golden brown, firm around the bottom edges, and starting to crack slightly, approximately 15 minutes.

13 Remove the pan from the oven and place on a cooling rack to cool for 1 hour.

14 When the logs are cool, place on a cutting surface. Using a serrated knife, slice the log on the diagonal into 1-inch (2.5 cm) pieces (h).

15 Lay the slices cut-side down on the parchment-lined pan and return to the oven (i).

16 Bake until the slices are toasted, approximately 10 to 12 minutes. Turn the slices over and toast the other side to the same color, approximately 8 to 10 minutes.

17 After the biscotti cool completely, you may dip them in tempered couverature (see page 27 for instructions on tempering chocolate).

a Combine the butter, sugar, and orange zest in the bowl of a stand mixer.

b Add the egg mixture to the butter mixture.

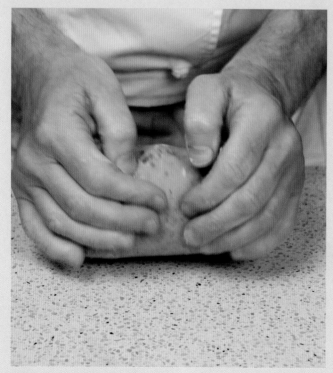

e Form the dough into logs.

f Roll logs to approximately 12 inches (30 cm).

c Add the coarsely chopped and toasted walnuts to the dough.

d Measure out 1-pound (455 g) portions of dough.

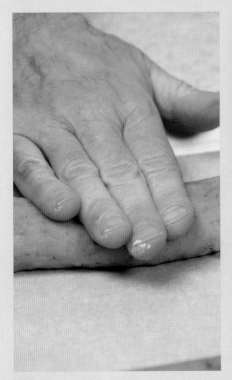

g Flatten the tops of the logs.

h Slice the logs on the diagonal into 1-inch (2.5 cm) pieces.

i Place the slices back on the pan, cut side down.

"A pastry chef is a passionate person with good taste, imagination, and creativity."

BUSINESS EXPERTS SAY THAT LUCK TRUMPS SMARTS EVERY TIME. IT DOESN'T HURT TO BE SMART, BUT LUCK CAN BE THE DIFFERENCE BETWEEN A DYNAMIC CAREER AND AN ORDINARY CAREER. FRIENDS AND COLLEAGUES OF FREDERIC DESHAYES AGREE THAT IT'S EVEN BETTER TO BE BOTH: LUCKY AND SMART.

FREDERIC DESHAYES,
CHIEF PASTRY & BAKERY INSTRUCTOR AT AT-SUNRICE GLOBALCHEF ACADEMY

A simple phone call was the beginning of the grand pastry tour that has been Frederic's career. He needed a job. He wanted a job making pastry. Although he had never heard of Lenotre—the godfather of modern French pastry—he liked their advertisement in the phone book. He dialed the number and was connected with the director of human resources and made an appointment. During his interview, Frederic and the HR director realized they were from the same town. A friendship was struck, and a career was born. Luck got him in the door; intelligence and hard work have guided him since, working for Lenotre in various capacities as well as a stint in Paris's venerable Plaza Athénée.

Frederic is approachable and friendly in his office and away from work. When he crosses the threshold of the pastry laboratory, however, his demeanor changes to that of a surgeon. He surveys the room, not seeking fault, but the opportunity to share his knowledge and experience. With masterful hands, keen understanding, and a few words, he mentors his staff and students in a positive, supportive environment. "Is this clean enough? Is this edge straight? May I show you? Do you see the difference? Now you do it." A few words, a brief demo, and he is off to the next student.

INTERVIEW WITH FREDERIC DESHAYES

YOUR FIRST AREA OF STUDY WAS CULINARY/SAVORY. HOW DID YOU MIGRATE FROM CULINARY TO PASTRY?

I had a strong interest in culinary by the time I was ten years old. In secondary school, we learned basic cooking and baking, which I enjoyed practicing at home. I always enjoyed helping my mother or my neighbor, who was a chef, prepare different dishes for barbecues and dinners.

By the time I was thirteen years old, I had failed my second year of secondary school. I had the choice of repeating the second year or attending a professional secondary school, LEP Lycee d'Enseignement Professionnel), a school with a culinary program near my home. I was selected for one of twenty-four places that year.

After three years, I completed my diploma in culinary arts. I was the youngest student in the class, and I had enough credits to graduate in the top five of my class. At sixteen, I graduated and should have been able to start to work. Unfortunately, I was too young to work under French law. I had developed an interest in pastry during the culinary program, so I decided to embark on a new journey as a student in pastry arts.

YOUR APPRENTICESHIP AND FIRST POSITION WERE WITH LENOTRE. WHAT WAS IT LIKE TO WORK FOR SUCH AN ICONIC ORGANIZATION?

After being accepted into the apprenticeship program, I was looking for a work site. There were no good pastry shops in my town, so I looked in the phone book

a site. I noticed a beautiful advertisement for a shop in a town near mine. It was for Lenotre. Of course, I had no idea what Lenotre was. I called to make appointment with human resources and the apprentice master. During the interview, the apprentice master commented that we were from the same town, and by the end of the interview I was selected to join the next group of Lenotre apprentices. Only ten apprentices are selected into the program per year.

There was no feeling of working in an industrial company. It was more like a family company where everyone knows each other. Once you are selected, you are a member of the family.

AT THE LENOTRE SHOP IN KOREA, WERE THE PASTRIES YOU MADE ADAPTED FOR LOCAL TASTES OR DID THEY REMAIN TRADITIONAL TO FRANCE?

Fifteen years ago, working in Korea was challenging due to the culture, the expectations in culinary taste, and the ingredients available. Franchised food chains had dominated the culinary landscape for so long that the pure tastes of our products were perceived as artificial. We started by reducing the sugar in the recipes and educating first our staff and then our customers about the quality of our ingredients and our techniques of production.

HOW DO THE DAY-TO-DAY OPERATIONS AS THE LEAD BAKING AND PASTRY INSTRUCTOR AT AT-SUNRICE DIFFER FROM THOSE OF A PASTRY CHEF IN A HOTEL OR PASTRY SHOP?

When you are a chef in a pastry shop or a hotel, you're in charge of the production of pastries, costs, the creation of new products. You are always able to adjust production to the abilities of your staff or the ingredients you can find. When you are a chef for a school, you are not producing tangible products but an intangible asset. We teach skills and knowledge, but we also show them our philosophy of what is possible in the culinary and pastry arts. When they graduate, our students should not just be two extra hands in the industry but an ambassador of the art and craft of pastry making.

WHAT IS MOST CHALLENGING ABOUT YOUR POSITION?

Meeting or exceeding the expectations of the directors and meeting the expectations of the students. Space is limited, time is limited, and both sides have reasonable yet high expectations.

HOW WOULD YOU DEFINE A PASTRY CHEF?

A pastry chef is a passionate person with good taste, imagination, and creativity.

WHAT IS YOUR PASTRY-MAKING STYLE?

Traditional pastries like I learned when I was an apprentice in Lenotre.

HOW DO YOU REMAIN MOTIVATED?

New challenges push you to maintain and improve skills, gain new knowledge, and observe what's happening around you.

OTHER THAN AN OVEN, WHICH ITEMS ARE ESSENTIAL TO EQUIP YOUR HOME KITCHEN?

A stand mixer; a saucepan; a whisk; a plastic, rubber, or stainless steel spatula; a digital scale; and a thermometer.

Chocolate/praline torte

WHAT WAS THE MOST DIFFICULT SKILL FOR YOU TO LEARN WHEN YOU WERE BEGINNING?

When I was training, my master told me the learning process for any skill has four stages:

See it, do it, understand how to do it, and know how to do it another way. The most difficult skill to learn at the beginning is being able to anticipate the requests of the chef, to know what he needs before he asks.

WHAT IS THE FIRST THING YOU TELL A NEW TEAM MEMBER OR STUDENT?

Any action has positive results or negative consequences. Think before acting.

WHAT ARE THE GUIDING RULES/ PRINCIPLES OF YOUR KITCHEN?

Don't always look for perfection; focus on the details.

WHAT DO YOU BAKE AT HOME?

In general I don't bake at home, but if I need to bake something it will be an apple tart or brownies. If we eat dessert at home, it is fresh fruit salad.

WHICH GIVES YOU MORE PLEASURE: MAKING PASTRY OR EATING PASTRY?

I have always enjoyed making pastry. In general I never eat them, except apple tarts and almond/pear tarts.

WHAT IS YOUR #1 STRENGTH AND YOUR BIGGEST WEAKNESS?

My strength is my ability to work with everything in the pastry arts, including yeasted products, tarts, *entremets*, ice cream, chocolate, confectionary, and sugar artistry. I seem to be able to adjust to any environment. My weakness is that I don't have strength in one specific area, and I have little imagination for creating new cakes or decorations.

WORDS TO LIVE BY?

Don't make excuses for your problems; find the solution. It's a big problem facing any industry: people who focus on excuses and let the responsibility of the solution to fall to others.

> *"New challenges push you to maintain and improve skills, gain new knowledge, and observe what's happening around you."*

Yield: 3 loaves (2 pounds, 3.3 ounces, or 1 kg each) or 30 muffins (3.6 ounces, or 100 g each)

Preparation time: active time, 20 minutes; total time 1¹/₂ to 1³/₄ hours

Equipment needed: Although this can be prepared manually, a stand mixer is recommended; microplane grater; sifter; 3 loaf pans

PAIN D'EPICES
BY FREDERIC DESHAYES

When the spice trade routes were first opened, *pain d'epices* was associated with the wealthier classes. It was a naturally leavened (sourdough) product containing little sugar. As sugar became more accessible, it was incorporated into the recipe. Over time, the bread has evolved to be more cakelike. The spice blend varies from region to region and from family to family. The only fat in the recipe is found in the egg yolk, yet the loaves remain tender and moist for a surprisingly long time. A favorite during the holiday season, it has become popular year round. Some chefs use it as a savory component, pairing it with strongly flavored items including foie gras and sausages.

INGREDIENTS

	U.S. Imperial Weight	Metric Weight	Volume
Whole wheat flour	7 oz	200 g	1¼ cups
Medium rye flour	24.7 oz	700 g	6½ cups
Baking powder	2.3 oz	65 g	5 tablespoons + 2 teaspoons
Allspice	0.2 oz	6 g	1 tablespoon
Cinnamon	1.1 oz	30 g	4 tablespoons + 2 teaspoons
Nutmeg	0.2 oz	6 g	1 tablespoon
Clove	0.07 oz	2 g	1 teaspoon
Ginger	0.1 oz	3 g	1¼ teaspoons
Black pepper	0.04 oz	1 g	¾ teaspoon
Whole milk			2 cups
Honey			2⅔ cups
Whole egg			12 eggs
Granulated sugar	6.4 oz	182 g	¾ cup + 2 tablespoons
Vanilla extract			3 teaspoons
Lemon zest	0.2 oz	6 g	1 tablespoon
Orange zest	0.2 oz	7 g	1 tablespoon
Salt	0.6 oz	18 g	1 tablespoon

PROCEDURE

1 Preheat oven to 325°F (170° C or gas mark 3).

2 Spray two 9 x 3 x 4-inch (23 x 7.5 x 10 cm) loaf pans with nonstick cooking spray. Line the bottom and short sides of pans with a strip of parchment paper to ensure the release of the baked product (a).

3 Combine and sift together flours, baking powder, allspice, cinnamon, nutmeg, ginger, and black pepper to ensure even distribution (b). Reserve.

4 Warm the milk and honey to 70° to 75°F (21° to 24°C) in a saucepan over low heat. The mixture will blend and homogenize more efficiently when the temperatures of the ingredients are equal. Reserve.

5 In the bowl of a stand mixer fitted with the whip attachment, whip the eggs and sugar to aerate, approximately 3 minutes.

6 Add the milk and honey to the whipped egg/sugar mixture. Whip lightly to combine.

7 Replace the whip attachment with the paddle attachment. (This helps prevent overaerating the batter, which would result in an overleavened product that might collapse, resulting in a gummy and doughy interior.)

8 Add flour mixture and mix on low just to combine. (Overmixing creates tough, rubbery loaves with tunnels in the interior.)

9 Evenly divide the batter between the prepared loaf pans (c). Use a disher (ice cream scoop) or other device to prevent splattering batter on the sides of the loaf pans, if desired.

10 Bake approximately 60 to 75 minutes. It will have a firm, browned crust that springs back when touched, and the sides of the loaf will have pulled away from the pan. Insert a clean skewer into the center of the loaf and remove it. If the skewer is clean, the cake is done.

11 Place the loaf pans on a cooling rack and leave for 10 to 15 minutes (d).

12 Invert the loaf pans to remove the loaves. Remove the parchment and return loaves to the cooling rack until completely cooled, allowing excess moisture to escape.

13 To bake muffins, preheat oven to 375°F (190°C or gas mark 5). Line the tins with paper liners, or spray the cavities and top surface of the tin liberally with nonstick cooking spray. Use a disher to fill the muffin cups to 75 percent of their capacity. Bake for 12 minutes; reduce the temperature to 350°F (180°C or gas mark 4) and continue baking until a skewer inserted in the muffin comes out clean, approximately 8 to 10 minutes. If liners are used, the muffins can cool in the pans for 10 minutes before removing. If liners are not used, remove the muffins directly after baking by tapping the sides of the muffin tin on a hard, clean surface. Place the muffins right side up on a cooling rack.

14 When cool, wrap the loaves or muffins in foil until you are ready to serve. Store at room temperature. The flavor fully diffuses and blooms on the second day—your patience will be rewarded.

Pain d'epices freezes well double wrapped in foil. Thaw at room temperature before serving.

This blending method is beneficial for recipes that contain a large percentage of liquids and oil as the type of fat used. With their high liquid content, cakes and quick breads made with this method remain moist and fresh for several days.

a Spray loaf pans with nonstick cooking spray and line with parchment paper.

b Combine the dry ingredients.

c Carefully pour the batter into the prepared pans.

d Let the pans cool slightly before removing the loaves.

IGINIO MASSARI MAKES TIME FOR EVERYONE. GENTLE, KIND, AND WARM, HIS PRESENCE IS GRANDFATHERLY AND AVUNCULAR; HE IS EVERYONE'S FAVORITE RELATIVE. HE IS A RACONTEUR AND A PHILOSOPHER OF ANOTHER ERA. THE GLEAM IN HIS EYES AND THE PASSION IN HIS VOICE ARE EVIDENCE OF THE LOVE OF BAKING HE HAS HAD FOR OVER FIFTY YEARS.

IGINIO MASSARI,
RESTAURATEUR AND FOUNDER OF THE ACADEMY OF ITALIAN MASTER PASTRY CHEFS

In Italy, where food is central to everyday living, he is a rock star. He goes to work at 4:30 every morning, frequently leaving at 11 p.m.; he says he is addicted to the work and the creativity. No aspect of the business is beyond his scope, be it bread, chocolate, showpieces, or pastry making. His books have been published in four languages and are considered bibles by many of the world's top pastry chefs and bakers.

He is a board member of Relais Dessert, the international organization committed to the highest level of pastry. His restaurants and pastry shops have received the top awards in Italy, and foreign governments, universities, and trade organizations have recognized him for his contributions to the industry.

"Happiness comes from working with your eyes and ears wide open."

INTERVIEW WITH IGINIO MASSARI

With appreciation to Biaggio Settepani, another great pastry chef, for translating

HOW WOULD YOU DESCRIBE A PASTRY CHEF?

A pastry chef expresses the intelligence of the hands together with the intelligence of the brain through the products he makes. You display the social and cultural aspects in addition to your personality through your work.

YOU ARE REGARDED AS A PASTRY CHEF, A CONFECTIONER, AND A BAKER. DID YOU BEGIN ALL THE SKILLS AT THE SAME TIME, OR DID YOU GRAVITATE FROM ONE TO THE OTHER?

My mother had a restaurant and a gelato shop. The aromas of my infancy remain in my mind. Restaurants are places where people gather and celebrate life. Gelato is the exclamation point.

After working in the family business, I was an apprentice in Switzerland. I worked in a pastry shop, a bakery, and in confectionary. This allowed me to create a solid foundation. The Swiss have excellent schools for teaching basics and fundamentals.

WHAT IS THE CURRENT MODEL IN ITALY FOR PEOPLE WISHING TO PURSUE A CAREER IN BAKING AND PASTRY? APPRENTICESHIP? SCHOOL? A MIXTURE?

The state school was converted to a private school, which I started. Now, every city has a culinary school. In 2010, there were 190,000 students across the country in culinary school. After grade school, young people can make a decision to attend these schools and choose to learn the back of the house or the front of the house.

DID YOU HAVE A MENTOR? ARE YOU STILL IN TOUCH WITH THAT PERSON?

A person that I particularly admired for his ability in Switzerland, Michel Gerber, was my mentor. His commitment to excellence as a professional and as a human being left a lifelong impression on me. In this profession, you are in contact with the public; it's more important to be a great person than a great baker or pastry chef.

AS THE FOUNDER AND DIRECTOR OF A SCHOOL, HOW DO YOU PERCEIVE THE DIFFERENCE BETWEEN EDUCATING SOMEONE AND TEACHING JOB SKILLS?

First, you have to be able to evaluate the passion. When I see a group of young people who are not professionals, I view them as sheep. The sheep stay with the other sheep. There is one student who is the dog that reins in the group. The student who becomes the shepherd guides that dog. He is the one that grows to be a proprietor and lead the group. Not everyone is a leader—the ones who avoid responsibility avoid life's daily competition. The World Pastry Cup happens every morning when you open the door. When I coach for the World Pastry Cup, I tell them every day: Why do you make a cake thirty times practicing for the World Pastry Cup and not give your clients the same attention and respect?

WHAT IS THE FIRST THING YOU SAY TO A STUDENT OR SOMEONE CONSIDERING BAKING AND PASTRY FOR A CAREER?

First, I look at them to see if they are stimulated and curious, and then I ask how important are holidays and weekends to them. I then ask them to read a few pages of a random book, because if they do not love to read, they do not have the inspiration or stimulation to be a leader. Another thing I look for is to see if they are willing to give up their personal taste in order to assume professional taste.

HOW HAS YOUR STYLE EVOLVED OVER TIME?

I try to renew the traditions. Every six months, I taste everything, reevaluate, and modify. I believe that in pastry, like in any other food-related industry, precision is paramount. That precision determines the final quality.

WHAT IS YOUR THOUGHT PROCESS WHEN CREATING A DESSERT MENU?

I think about the seasons, even though there are no more seasons. We have everything all year. You do not perceive the extraordinary aroma and taste of the fruit because it is no longer special and it is grown under less-than-desirable conditions. I notice that 85 percent of people do not understand the balance between flavors and taste. Globally, [professionals] confuse taste and flavor. Now it is in style to add salt to chocolate. In its natural state, chocolate is bitter, sweet, and acidic. In the last few years, salt has appeared in everything. Why?

OTHER THAN BUTTER, FLOUR, SUGAR, EGGS, AND SALT, WHAT ARE THE FIRST TEN INGREDIENTS YOU WOULD SELECT FOR YOUR KITCHEN?

It is difficult to exclude anything. We should all know the four basic ingredients: flour; liquid, including eggs (structure); fats (butter); and sugar to create quality. You could produce 100 basic recipes, and through manipulation you could get multiple effects. Baking temperatures and handling create big variations on an incredible physical level. Few people research this. For cooking meat, you need a sharp eye as opposed to the science and precision of the pastry chef. In restaurants, execution is sensory, not scientific.

OTHER THAN AN OVEN, WHICH ITEMS ARE ESSENTIAL TO EQUIP YOUR HOME KITCHEN?

The essentials are a small stand mixer and a scale.

WHAT ARE THE GUIDING PRINCIPLES/RULES OF YOUR KITCHEN?

Concentration, silence, cleanliness, precision, general respect.

WHAT TYPES OF PASTRIES/ DESSERTS ARE MADE IN THE TYPICAL ITALIAN HOME?

Generally, the biggest consumption of desserts is on the weekend when we entertain or visit others. Panettone is the most-consumed dessert. At one time, it symbolized social status. Since 1945, people have forgotten its significance. When you give panettone as a gift, the raisins represent wealth, the candied orange represents love, and the citron represents eternity. Industrialization changed this. Only numbers matter. In Italy, all the sweets have a symbolic message. Very few professionals are aware of the history and tradition. Yet the history persists.

IF YOU HAD TO CHOOSE BETWEEN ONLY EATING PASTRIES OR ONLY MAKING PASTRIES, WHICH WOULD YOU CHOOSE?

Making pastries and letting everyone else enjoy them.

WHAT IS YOUR GREATEST STRENGTH? WHAT IS YOUR BIGGEST WEAKNESS?

My strength is my curiosity. My weakness is saying yes to everything. I don't know how to say no.

HOW DO YOU STAY MOTIVATED?

It's a question I ask myself. At night, I ask why. In the morning I am charged. I must have brain damage.

WHAT ARE YOUR GOALS FOR THE FUTURE?

To create an international pastry guide similar to the Michelin guide for restaurants in order to stimulate the industry. In France, they have MOF. In Italy, I am going to create MPI, which will be approved by the government. I am scheduled to meet with the labor minister of Italy to organize MPI. We will establish standards for converting regional pastries into national pastries. I also plan to build a complete glossary, creating a manual that explains in full detail what equipment, ingredients, and techniques are used. And finally, a reference for defining all the pastries.

WHAT ARE YOUR WORDS TO LIVE BY?

Sacrifice does not exist. What exists is something that you are forced to do against your will. In Catholicism, if someone would have to crawl across the continent, he would arrive with his knees ground down to the bone and in enormous pain. This would not be a sacrifice because you realized your goal. If you work according to the social stature, you will be rewarded with happiness. Happiness is conjugated with the verb being. I'm happy, you're happy; things are not happy. Happiness comes from working with your eyes and ears wide open.

Yield: One 10 x 2-inch (25 x 5 cm) cake

Preparation time: active time, 20 minutes; total time, 12 to 18 hours

Equipment needed: Although this can be mixed by hand, a stand mixer will take less time and enable the baker to attend to other tasks at the same time; cake pan; box grater.

SBRISOLONA
BY IGINIO MASSARI

Sbrisolona originated in rural Italy and symbolizes seasonal and economic recovery. It was a neighborly exchange between farmers' families, who would gather and compare their individual cakes. It was traditionally made in November after the harvest, around the same time the new wines debuted. With its dry texture, Sbrisolona is perfect for dipping in wine. The different family wines and Sbrisolonas were paired and judged by all the families—not in a contentious manner, but certainly a highly competitive one. The fat used to make the cake was reserved and strained after frying and roasting family meals in pans. In the countryside, nothing was discarded. The different fats provided distinctive, pungent, and aromatic flavors. Whether it was chicken, beef, pork, game, fowl, or a combination of fats, the flavors contributed to the individuality of the cakes.

INGREDIENTS

	U.S. Imperial Weight	Metric Weight	Volume
Bread flour*	14.1 oz	400 g	3 cups + 2 tablespoons
Corn flour**	3.5 oz	100 g	¾ cup + ½ teaspoon
Baking powder	.4 oz	10 g	1 tablespoon + 1 teaspoon
Almond flour	3.5 oz	100 g	¾ cup + ½ teaspoon
Vanilla bean, scraped	1 bean	1 bean	1 bean
Unsalted butter, cubed***	8.8 oz	250 g	1 cup
Granulated sugar	7 oz	200 g	1 cup
Salt	0.1 oz	2.5 g	¾ teaspoon
Whole egg			½ egg
Egg yolk			1½ yolks
Grand Marnier			3 teaspoons
Ammonium bicarbonate****	0.18 oz	5 g	2 teaspoons
Water			2 teaspoons
Confectioners' sugar, for dusting			

Recipe notes:

*Protein level 11%–12%

**Masa harina

***Use European-style butter (minimum 82% fat content)

****Available from baking supplies specialist or ethnic markets

PROCEDURE

1 In the bowl of a stand mixer fitted with a paddle attachment, blend the bread flour, corn flour, baking powder, almond flour, vanilla scrapings, and cubed butter lightly. The mixture should be a rough, shaggy mass.

2 Add the sugar, salt, egg, egg yolk, and Grand Marnier and mix lightly.

3 Dissolve the ammonium bicarbonate in the water and add to the dough.

4 Mix lightly until the dough is uniform (a).

5 Place on a lightly floured work surface and form into a tight ball.

6 Flatten the ball and wrap the dough in plastic wrap. Refrigerate overnight.

7 The next day, preheat the oven to 350°F (175°C or gas mark 4).

8 Butter a 10 x 2-inch (25.4 x 5 cm) cake pan and line with parchment (b).

9 Remove the dough from the refrigerator and crumble (c). Use the largest holes on a box grater if necessary.

10 Without packing or compacting them, gently place the crumbles in the buttered and lined cake pan (d).

11 Place the Sbrisolona in the oven and bake until golden brown and a toothpick inserted in the cake comes out clean, approximately 30 to 40 minutes (e).

12 Remove from the oven and dust with confectioners' sugar (f).

13 Reserve at room temperature until served. Stored in an airtight container, it remains fresh for several days. Older Sbrisolona is dipped in coffee, tea, hot chocolate, or wine.

a Note the texture of the finished dough.

d Gently pour the crumbles into the prepared pan.

The rubbing method coats the particles of flour with fat, making them impermeable to water and reducing the likelihood of gluten development, resulting in tender products. Although there is very little water in Sbrisolona, the rubbing method is used to make a cake that more closely resembles crumble topping or streusel. The major difference in Sbrisolona dough and streusel is the addition of the chemical leavening agents baking powder and ammonium bicarbonate.

b Line the cake pan with parchment.

c Crumble the dough.

e Bake until golden brown.

f Dust with confectioners' sugar.

Ammonium bicarbonate is used in drier baked goods. Due to the fact that there is not enough moisture in the dough to activate the leavening, it is necessary to dissolve ammonium bicarbonate in water to activate it. The amount of gas released is very strong, and the odor is startling if inhaled directly. It is not harmful, but slightly unpleasant—exercise caution when working with it.

AS THE PASTRY CHEF FOR THE THOMAS KELLER RESTAURANT GROUP, SÉBASTIEN ROUXEL OVERSEES ALL PASTRIES PRODUCED AT ALL NINE VENUES, INCLUDING THE FRENCH LAUNDRY AND AD HOC IN YOUNTVILLE, CALIFORNIA, AND PER SE AND BOUCHON IN NEW YORK CITY.

SÉBASTIEN ROUXEL,
EXECUTIVE PASTRY CHEF FOR THE THOMAS KELLER RESTAURANT GROUP

When he was sixteen, Sébastien, a native of the Loire Valley in France, began a culinary apprenticeship on the savory line of a Michelin-starred restaurant. While working there, he discovered his passion for making pastries. He transferred to another restaurant to intern as a pastry cook. Within two years, he received his master's degree.

By the time he was twenty years old, Sébastien was the executive pastry chef at the Mess de L'Elysée, the official residence of the French president. After serving his country, Sébastien was the pastry chef at the three-Michelin-star restaurant Le Grand Véfour in Paris. In the United States, he served as pastry chef at L'Orangerie and Lutec before joining the Thomas Keller Group in 1999. In 2005, he was named a Rising Star, and in 2005 and 2008 he was recognized as one of the Top Ten Pastry Chefs in America by *Dessert Professional* magazine.

A gentleman in the kitchen, Sébastien teaches professionalism, food knowledge, ethics, and skills with the same precision and determination he harnesses to create new desserts for the establishments that are regarded as America's best restaurants.

"Dessert is a way to express yourself as an artist does—le patissier uses techniques, colors, shapes, and imagination under a rigorous and mathematic set of rules in ways that are diverse and also precise."

WHICH SKILL WAS MOST DIFFICULT FOR YOU TO LEARN AS A BEGINNER?

Like most beginners, I wanted to see and learn something new every day. I was eager to learn new recipes and didn't want to fill 300 pieces of *pâte à choux* every day. I realize that consistency and to be able to execute the same thing every day the same or better is one of the most difficult skills to learn and to teach to the new generation. Consistency is also a key asset for the success of a business.

OTHER THAN AN OVEN, WHICH ITEMS ARE ESSENTIAL TO EQUIP YOUR HOME KITCHEN?

For me, a kitchen must have the following items: a good scale, a stand mixer, a half sheet pan (or full size if your oven allows), a whisk, a palette knife or spatula, and a knife.

INTERVIEW WITH SÉBASTIEN ROUXEL

ARE THERE DIFFERENCES BETWEEN HOME COOKS IN FRANCE AND OUTSIDE OF FRANCE? DIFFERENCES BETWEEN PROFESSIONALS?

From my point of view, I would say that the main difference is food knowledge, education, and culture. France has had an extensive cuisine evolution over centuries. Everyone there is exposed to food at an early age and goes to the *boulangerie/patisserie* to buy their daily bread and pastries, to the butcher to buy meat, etc. It is an almost sacred routine. Meals are important, and they take the time to eat and to make home-cooked meals. Professionally, becoming a chef is a passion, a lifestyle, and/or something you grew up within

DESCRIBE YOUR STYLE OR PHILOSOPHY.

La patisserie is a world of its own, an adventure. It is also a place where all your senses are challenged and pleased. Each sense connects to the next, and we experience a firework of impressions that will fulfill us. Dessert is the jewel that we looked for or craved as children, either from passing by the pastry shop on our way home from school or that we were served after eating our meal. Dessert is a way to express yourself as an artist does—*le patissier* uses techniques, colors, shapes, and imagination under a rigorous and mathematic set of rules in ways that are diverse and also precise.

IF YOU HAD TO CHOOSE BETWEEN ONLY EATING OR ONLY MAKING PASTRIES, WHICH WOULD YOU CHOOSE AND WHY?

I love to eat, so if I had to choose, I probably would go with eating. I love food, and having to give that up doesn't seem right. I'm always looking forward to dinner with my loved ones.

WHAT IS YOUR THOUGHT PROCESS WHEN WRITING A PASTRY MENU?

To me, the art of making dessert/pastry for a restaurant or a pastry shop is to be able to complement and to continue the tone that the chef has or the business model

Macaron Royal

Black Pearl

Spiced Caramel and Pear Duo

WHAT ARE THE GUIDING PRINCIPLES/RULES OF YOUR KITCHEN?

The first rule is our dress code. We have specifics, and we ask that each staff member follow them (or they get sent home). We also have a set of core values that we expect the staff to follow and live by while working. All employees are responsible for the cleanliness of the pastry department, both continually during their working period and at the end of shift break down. All employees are responsible for looking after and treating our equipment with respect in order to ensure it's in good working order. We require our employees to work with focus, finesse, and a sense of urgency. They should be constantly looking for and thinking about their current task, next task, and the rest of their workload in order to increase productivity and create a professional working environment.

HOW DO YOU STAY MOTIVATED?

I have been fortunate and came across some great challenges. I love what I do, and I want to perform and do the best I can. I try to stay updated with what is going on in the pastry world.

DESCRIBE YOUR IDEAL PASTRY VACATION.

Right now, it would probably be a trip across Europe (France, Italy, Spain) visiting and tasting reputable establishments with some of my peers.

WORDS TO LIVE BY?

Perseverance, consistency, quality, and discipline.

"*I realize that consistency and to be able to execute the same thing every day the same or better is one of the most difficult skills to learn and to teach to the new generation. Consistency is also a key asset for the success of a business.*"

PÂTE À CHOUX
BY SÉBASTIEN ROUXEL

Pâte à choux is a unique amalgam that is neither dough nor batter. The flour is cooked prior to baking, which swells and gelatinizes the starches. It is leavened by steam generated from the water in milk and eggs. Apprentices practice mixing, baking, and piping it thousands of times, and a great variety of pastries are made from this simple preparation.

INGREDIENTS

	U.S. Imperial Weight	Metric Weight	Volume
Water			5½ cups
Unsalted butter*	1 lb, 5 oz	595 g	2¼ cups + 1 tablespoon
Granulated sugar	3.5 oz	100 g	½ cup
Salt	0.6 oz	18 g	1 tablespoon
Bread flour	1 lb, 15 oz	879 g	6¼ cups + ⅓ cup
Whole egg			25 eggs
Engadine nuss torte dough (for cream puffs) See recipe, page 76			1 recipe

Recipe note: Use European-style butter (minimum 82% fat content).

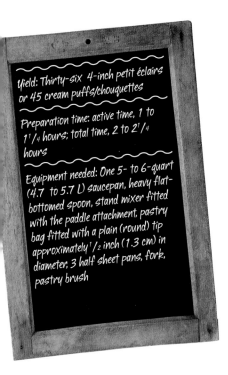

Yield: Thirty-six 4-inch petit éclairs
or 45 cream puffs/chouquettes

Preparation time: active time, 1 to
1 1/4 hours; total time, 2 to 2 1/4
hours

Equipment needed: One 5- to 6-quart
(4.7 to 5.7 L) saucepan, heavy flat-
bottomed spoon, stand mixer fitted
with the paddle attachment, pastry
bag fitted with a plain (round) tip
approximately 1/2 inch (1.3 cm) in
diameter, 3 half sheet pans, fork,
pastry brush

PROCEDURE (see photos, page 58–60)

1 In a heavy-bottomed pot, combine the water, butter, sugar, and salt and bring to a boil (a).

2 Remove the pot from the stove and add the flour all at once.

3 Using a heavy, flat-bottomed spoon, mix well and return the pot to the stove. Cook until the mixture forms a smooth paste and cleans the sides of the pot (referred to as panade). This swells and gelatinizes the starch in the flour, helping to set the structure of the shells (b).

4 Transfer the mixture to the bowl of a stand mixer fitted with the paddle attachment.

5 Mix on medium speed. Move the flame of a torch around the bottom of the exterior surface of the bowl for a few seconds to expel excess moisture, if necessary.

6 Continue mixing and incorporate the eggs one at a time, pausing between additions to permit full incorporation. The paste should be fluid and viscous when all of the egg has been incorporated (c).

7 Allow the mixture to cool to room temperature before piping so the pieces will retain their shape.

8 Deposit the mixture in a pastry bag fitted with a plain round tip approximately ½ inch (1.3 cm) in diameter, filling the bag 60 percent full. Twist the open end of the bag tightly, closing it to prevent the mixture from working its way out of the rear of the bag as you pipe.

9 Line a sheet pan with parchment or a silicone baking mat. To pipe cream puffs and/or chouquettes, hold the bag perpendicular to and slightly above the prepared sheet pan. Holding the bag stationary, apply even pressure until the surface of the piped shape is touching the tip. Release the pressure and remove the tip (d).

10 To pipe éclairs, hold the tip at a 45° angle slightly above the prepared sheet pan. Apply even pressure while pulling back on the bag. Use a similar technique to pipe other shapes (e, f).

11 If time permits, freeze the shapes before baking. Otherwise, refrigerate for a minimum of one hour.

12 Preheat the oven to 350°F (180°C or gas mark 4).

13 Remove the sheet pans from the freezer and brush the shapes with egg (g). For cream puffs (round shapes), place a thin, small disc of engadine nuss torte dough (see page 76) on the moistened surface (h). For chouquettes, another Parisian treat, sprinkle the egg-washed rounds liberally with *sucre grain* (pearl sugar). Use granulated sugar if pearl sugar is unavailable.

14 Place the pastry shapes in the preheated oven and reduce the heat to 330°F (170°C or gas mark 3).

15 Bake until the shapes are golden brown and no moisture is visible on the surface, approximately 18 to 22 minutes. To double-check for doneness, hold one of the shapes to your ear. If you hear hissing, the moisture has not been fully expelled, and the pastry shells are not done. Continue baking until there is no sound coming from the shells.

16 Cool completely before cutting and/or filling.

17 To fill the cream puffs, use a serrated knife to remove and reserve the top portion.

18 Using a pastry bag fitted with a star tip, fill the cavity with crème Chantilly (see page 17) (i). (Optional: place a small amount of pastry cream [see page 103] in the bottom of the cavity before piping in the crème Chantilly.)

(continued)

PROCEDURE (continued)

19 Place the cut tops on top of the filling.

20 Sift confectioners' sugar over the surface of the cream puffs and refrigerate until service. If refrigerated for a lengthy period of time, the puffs may require a second sifting of sugar.

21 To fill the éclairs, use the tip of a paring knife to cut a small hole in each half of the bottom of the éclair.

22 Using a pastry bag fitted with a plain (round) tip, fill the éclairs with pastry cream (j).

23 Dip the éclairs into tempered couverature (see page 27 for instructions on tempering chocolate) and refrigerate until service.

24 Assemble other desired shapes, if using (k).

Pâte à choux may be baked and frozen for up to five weeks for future use. Place the cooled shells in a resealable plastic freezer bag and seal. Place the bag in another resealable plastic freezer bag and seal. To use, remove the shells from the bag, place on a parchment-lined sheet pan, and thaw at room temperature for 30 to 40 minutes. Proceed as directed.

Shells made from pâte à choux are frequently used for savory appetizers and *amuse bouches*. They are split and filled with prepared items such as pâté, chicken salad, tuna salad, etc. A classic French potato preparation, *pommes de terre dauphinoise* is made by blending equal parts pâte à choux and puréed potato. Quenelles, or dumplings, are formed and deep fried.

a Bring the water, butter, sugar, and salt to a boil.

d Pipe the dough into round shapes for cream puffs.

b Cook until dough pulls away from the sides of the pot.

c Note the consistency of the final dough.

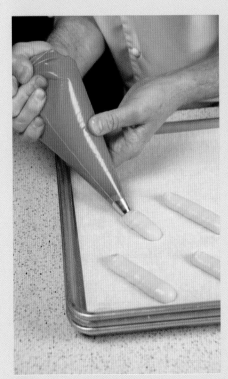

e Pipe the dough in straight lines for éclairs.

f Pipe the dough into shapes, if desired.

g Brush the dough with egg wash or water.

(continued)

h Top the cream puffs with a disc of *pâte sucree*.

i Fill the cream puffs with crème Chantilly.

j Fill the éclairs with pastry cream.

k Assemble desired shapes using crème Chantilly to hold pieces in place.

AFTER GRADUATING FROM SKIDMORE COLLEGE WITH PHOTOGRAPHY AND JEWELRY DESIGN CONCENTRATIONS, EN-MING, A NATIVE OF VIRGINIA, WASTED LITTLE TIME IN APPLYING TO THE CULINARY INSTITUTE OF AMERICA. SHE ENROLLED IN THE CULINARY PROGRAM; HOWEVER, SHORTLY AFTER BEGINNING HER STUDIES, SHE HEARD OF A NEW PROGRAM AT THE SCHOOL: BAKING AND PASTRY. SHE ENROLLED AND WAS THE FIRST PERSON TO GRADUATE FROM THE CIA WITH A DEGREE IN BAKING AND PASTRY ARTS

EN-MING HSU,
WORLD CHAMPION CONSULTANT AND CHEF INSTRUCTOR AT THE FRENCH PASTRY SCHOOL IN CHICAGO

The first few years of her new career were spent in fine dining restaurants in New York City and Washington DC. Her next job as the executive pastry chef of the Ritz-Carlton in Chicago is the one that put her on an international stage. While working there, she won the Patisfrance Pastry Chef of the Year competition, was named one of the Top Ten Pastry Chefs in America twice, and captained the U.S. team to the gold medal at the *Coupe du Monde de la Patisserie*. In July 2010, she was recognized as the Pastry Chef of the Year during the World Pastry Team Championship.

Currently, she is a faculty member of the French Pastry School in Chicago and maintains a consulting business based in Las Vegas.

"When cooks start in the field, they must be patient and take the time to learn and grow. Culinary schools arm them with knowledge for basic preparations and methods. Each work experience will allow them to build on that foundation. If they are dedicated and focused, they will excel. They must remember that it takes time."

INTERVIEW WITH EN-MING HSU

DESCRIBE YOUR STYLE AND PHILOSOPHY OF PASTRY MAKING.

My style is conservative, simple, and classic. I enjoy taking traditional methods or flavor combinations and working with them. I search for unique ingredients and incorporate them into my recipes. The flow of courses from start to finish is important to me. I like bringing savory elements or cooking techniques into the recipes, as well. Most important is the use of fresh local ingredients whenever possible and complementing their flavors. I have a growing interest and understanding of sustainable agriculture and the importance of sourcing our foods.

WHAT SPARKS YOUR IMAGINATION AND INSPIRES YOU?

My biggest inspiration is the food product itself, taking the time to understand the ingredients we use. When I find a beautiful piece of fruit, I create the dessert around it. I also find inspirations by paying attention to what consumers like. It doesn't necessarily mean I will follow along with all current trends, but I will take note of what is happening. Farmers and producers are very inspirational.

WHAT ARE THE GUIDING PRINCIPLES/RULES OF YOUR KITCHEN?

Treat everyone in the kitchen with respect regardless of his or her position, but recognize rank. Give credit where it is due. I believe I am very fair in the kitchen. I want the cooks to have an opinion and learn to think for themselves. But there can only be one chef, so there has to be a balance. I have high expectations of everyone and like to see them reach their potential.

OTHER THAN BUTTER, FLOUR, SUGAR, EGGS, AND SALT, WHAT ARE THE FIRST TEN INGREDIENTS YOU WOULD SELECT FOR YOUR KITCHEN?

Chocolate 65 percent, milk, heavy cream, cornstarch, lemons, almonds, cream of tartar, baking soda, Cassia cinnamon or Bourbon vanilla beans (I can't decide), and wildflower honey. With these ingredients, I can combine some of them to create other stock ingredients (for example, baking soda + cream of tartar + cornstarch = baking powder) and expand my basic pantry.

OTHER THAN AN OVEN, WHAT ARE THE WISEST EQUIPMENT CHOICES FOR THE BEGINNING PASTRY CHEF?

A stand mixer, an immersion blender, a microplane grater, a whisk, a rubber spatula, and a French knife.

AS A CONSUMER, DESCRIBE YOUR IDEAL PASTRY VACATION.

I had one once. For many years, I collected articles and read about pastry shops and chocolatiers in Paris. When I went to École Lenotre outside of Paris for classes, I stayed in Paris for a few days after. I went to every pastry and chocolate shop on that list (dragging my husband along). It was unbelievable.

WHAT IS YOUR THOUGHT PROCESS WHEN WRITING A DESSERT MENU?

I look first at the balance of the dessert varieties. The balance is for flavor—chocolate desserts, seasonal fruit desserts, frozen desserts, custard desserts, something with an interesting ingredient. I look at the "weight" of the items (richer or lighter, temperatures) too. I consider the amount of time it takes to prep the desserts and balance which take more or less time. I look at the amount of time needed to fire the dessert (imagining the worst-case scenario with 20 tickets on the board). I look at food cost, too. I offset expensive desserts with lower-cost items.

Black Forest tower with sweet black cherries and chocolate cremeux

Wildflower honey yogurt panna cotta with elderflower gelee and red berry salad

WHAT IS THE BEST ADVICE YOU HAVE RECEIVED?

After I graduated from college, I was working on my portfolio to go to graduate school for jewelry design. I had a hard time finishing it (remember, I wanted to go to cooking school). I had been working with my college jewelry professor, who really wanted me to pursue the degree. Finally, he said I should try the cooking route "because we all have to eat. We don't have to wear jewelry." The other piece that I always remember: A good pastry chef always keeps something up his or her sleeve. That came from Markus Farbinger, one of my chef instructors at the CIA.

HOW DO YOU STAY MOTIVATED?

When I see what [other chefs in the industry are] doing, it reminds me of how complex and exciting our business is. I work with many other chefs in different environments worldwide and find a lot of stimulation from that.

WHAT WAS THE MOST DIFFICULT THING FOR YOU TO LEARN WHEN YOU WERE BEGINNING?

The most difficult to learn was how to work more efficiently and manage my time. As a perfectionist, it was hard to know when to stop doing something and move on. I'm sure that drove some of my chefs crazy. As I understood more, it became easier to streamline production and think for myself and manage a prep list. It's easy to prioritize now.

WHAT IS YOUR #1 STRENGTH?

My strength is my true passion for the work that I do. If I did not have that, I don't think I would have stayed in this business. I would either become disinterested or burned out. I continue to explore and learn about different facets of our field.

WHAT DO YOU BAKE AT HOME?

I used to bake a lot more for home, but not so much now because we are not at home much. My husband is a chef, too. If we have friends over, we will have fun cooking. If I'm lucky and there are fruits to harvest from my backyard, I'll make an apricot, peach, or fig tart. If I have time, I'll make fresh cheese, like *fromage blanc*, and serve it with figs or grapes. I usually keep some doughs or crumble toppings in the freezer. I can very quickly make a baked crumble to serve with ice cream.

WHAT ADVICE DO YOU HAVE FOR NEW CHEFS?

When cooks start in the field, they must be patient and take the time to learn and grow. Culinary schools arm them with knowledge for basic preparations and methods. Each work experience will allow them to build on that foundation. If they are dedicated and focused, they will excel. They must remember that it takes time.

DISCUSS PUFF PASTRY'S CHARACTERISTICS, VERSATILITY, AND PLACE IN THE REPERTOIRE.

Puff pastry is a dough that many kitchens use in savory and sweet recipes, but few kitchens make it from scratch. Professional and home kitchens can buy it in all forms for a reasonable cost. Puff pastry can be bought as laminated books or sheets, pre-cut or shaped. Some are made with butter and some with vegetable fats, so the cost fits all budgets. It is a staple in the kitchen because of its versatility. If it is well made, puff pastry is rich and buttery, texturally interesting, and ideal for many recipes. It also freezes well, so when properly stored, it is convenient to use. Pastry chefs should understand how to make basic recipes like puff pastry. It is amazing what can be done with flour, water, and butter, especially if we understand how to manipulate the ingredients. In puff pastry, we want to create layers of crispy dough. The bite is tender and flaky. Using a lower-protein flour leads to less gluten development, so the results are not tough.

Butter surrounds the flour particles to inhibit gluten development when water is added. It also ensures tenderness. Adding vinegar to acidify the water also helps by breaking down the gluten proteins. If the temperature of the room and ingredients are ideal (65–68°F [18–20°C]), it is easy to make. The goal is to not overwork the dough to make sure the layers are distributed so they rise evenly. The number of turns is based on the results desired. More turns create layers that are more compact, while fewer turns create flakier, higher layers.

WORDS TO LIVE BY?

Try not to focus on success. Make yourself significant to others and the success will come to you.

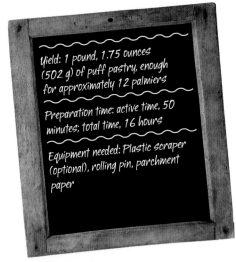

Yield: 1 pound, 1.75 ounces (502 g) of puff pastry, enough for approximately 12 palmiers

Preparation time: active time, 50 minutes; total time, 16 hours

Equipment needed: Plastic scraper (optional), rolling pin, parchment paper

PUFF PASTRY
BY EN-MING HSU

Puff pastry is the base for many traditional and contemporary pastries. The lamination process alternates layers of dough and layers of butter, resulting in a flaky pastry. European-style butter with its higher fat content (reduced water content) is easier to work with and provides better layering. Puff pastry is the base for Napoleons, *pithiviers*, the popular *tarte tatin,* and the Palmiers that follow. Its neutral buttery flavor renders it equally useful for savory applications.

INGREDIENTS

	U.S. Imperial Weight	Metric Weight	Volume
Pastry flour	7.1 oz	200 g	1¾ cups + 1 tablespoon
Unsalted butter*	0.9 oz	25 g	5½ teaspoons
Cold water			½ cup minus 1 tablespoon
Distilled vinegar			2 ml
Salt	0.2 oz	5 g	⅝ teaspoon
Unsalted butter*	6.2 oz	175 g	1¼ cups

Recipe note: Use European-style butter (minimum 82% fat content).

PROCEDURE

1 On a flat work surface, mound the flour and make a well in the center (a).

2 Melt the 0.9 ounce (25 g) of butter until it just begins to soften; it should be viscous, not liquid.

3 Combine the water and vinegar. Add the salt and stir well to dissolve.

4 Pour the vinegar mixture and the viscous butter into the well in the center of the flour (b).

5 Using your fingertips, gradually work the flour into the liquid, using a plastic scraper to assist if necessary (c).

6 Form the dough into a rough ball, then flatten it, forming a rectangle (d).

7 Wrap the dough in plastic and refrigerate for a minimum of 2 hours.

8 Thirty minutes prior to laminating the dough, pound the 6.2 ounces (175 g) of butter until it is pliable (e). Your goal is to make the butter and the dough the same consistency, not necessarily the same temperature. The butter should be malleable so it can be extended between the layers of dough and so it can be folded.

9 Fold a long rectangle of parchment paper in half (f).

10 With the short side of the parchment facing you, fold down the top and bottom so that the center (unfolded part) measures approximately 7.5 inches (19.5 cm) (g).

11 Rotate the parchment 90 degrees, then fold in the top and bottom so the center (unfolded part) measures approximately 4.5 inches (11.5 cm) (h).

12 Unfold the parchment and place the softened butter in the center of the rectangle formed by the creases that is closest to you (i).

13 Fold the parchment over the butter and refold the creases to seal the envelope (j).

14 Smooth out the butter packet with a rolling pin and refrigerate until needed (k).

15 When ready, remove the dough from the refrigerator and place on a lightly floured work surface.

16 Using a rolling pin, shape the dough into a 5- x 12-inch (13 x 30.5 cm) rectangle.

(continued)

PROCEDURE (continued)

17 Remove the butter from the parchment envelope and place it on top of the dough, covering two-thirds of the surface (l).

18 Fold the uncovered dough over half of the butter. Using a dry brush, remove the excess flour from the dough (m).

19 Fold the remaining third of the dough (covered with butter) over the previous fold, as if folding a business letter. Use a dry brush to remove the excess flour. Manipulate the dough if necessary to ensure that the butter is completely encased (n).

20 Wrap in plastic and refrigerate the dough for a minimum of 15 minutes.

21 Remove the dough from the refrigerator and place it on a lightly floured work surface with the exposed (short) end nearest you.

22 Using a rolling pin, elongate the rectangle to 5 x 12 inches (13 x 30.5 cm). Roll evenly and efficiently to avoid overmanipulating the dough.

23 Repeat the folding process as described above.

24 Wrap in plastic and refrigerate the dough for a minimum of 30 minutes.

25 Repeat steps 17 through 19 two more times.

26 Refrigerate the dough for 2 hours.

27 Remove the dough from the refrigerator and repeat the rolling and folding process.

28 Wrap in plastic and refrigerate overnight.

29 The following day, remove the dough from the refrigerator and repeat the rolling and folding process one final time.

30 Refrigerate for a minimum of 1 hour.

Butter is most plastic (pliable) between 60–70°F (16–21°C). It is soft at 80°F (21°C). It has a melting point of 88°F (31°C), and due to the different crystals in its composition, it has a final melting point of 94°F (34°C). If the butter is too soft or melts during any part of the process, the layers will be lost, along with the flaky characteristic of the puff pastry. If the butter is too cold, it will shatter during the process, resulting in uneven lamination.

Layers of dough separated by layers of butter create light and flaky pastry. To create and maintain adequate layering (called lamination), the butter and the dough should be the same consistency. Most home refrigerators have an internal temperature of approximately 40°F (4.4°C). At that temperature, butter is hard, while dough remains malleable. Removing the butter from the refrigerator a few minutes prior to beginning the lamination procedure ensures that the dough and the butter will be the same consistency, ideal for effective lamination.

a Make a well in the center of the flour.

e Pound the butter with a rolling pin until it's softened.

b Pour the liquids into the well.

c Gently mix until dough comes together and is smooth.

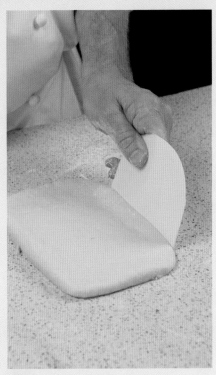

d Form the dough into a rectangle.

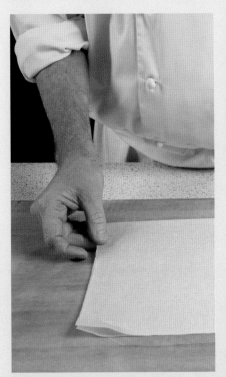

f Fold a long rectangle of parchment in half.

g Fold the top and bottom so that the center measures approximately 7.5 inches (19.5 cm).

h Rotate the parchment 90°. Fold in the top and bottom so the center measures approximately 4.5 inches (11.5 cm).

(continued)

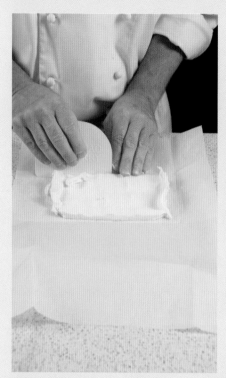

i Place the malleable butter in the envelope.

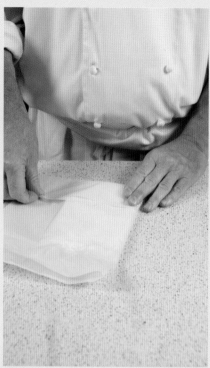

j Fold the parchment over the butter and refold the creases to seal.

k Gently roll the surface to smooth out the butter.

l Place the butter rectangle on top of the dough.

m Use a dry brush to remove excess flour.

n Fold the butter-covered third over the previous fold.

Yield: 12 palmiers

Preparation time: active time,
20 minutes; total time 40 minutes.

Equipment needed: Rolling pin, sharp
knife, parchment paper, sheet pan.

PALMIERS
BY EN-MING HSU

Palmiers are crisp, light, flaky, and sweet without being gooey. They are considered *petit fours sec*—dry petit fours. They are served with coffee and tea as well as by themselves. They frequently appear with other dry petit fours on buffets and *mingmardise* platters. They are best when served fresh; freezing will cause them to lose some of their crispiness.

INGREDIENTS

	U.S. Imperial Weight	Metric Weight	Volume
Puff pastry dough	1 recipe	1 recipe	1 recipe
Flour, for work surface			
Sugar, for sprinkling			

PROCEDURE (see photos, page70–71)

1 Preheat oven to 375°F (190°C or gas mark 5).

2 Remove the dough from the refrigerator and place on a lightly floured work surface.

3 Using a rolling pin, extend the dough until into a rectangle until it is approximately ⅛ inch (0.3 cm) thick and approximately 16 inches (40.6 cm) by 10 inches (25.4 cm).

4 Just before the dough is the proper thickness, clear the work surface of flour and cover it with sugar. Sprinkle the top of the dough with sugar (a).

5 Extend the dough to the proper thickness.

6 Fold the edge of the dough facing you one-quarter of the way toward the center (b).

7 Fold again, ending with the folded edge in the center of the dough.

8 Fold the opposite edge of the dough one-quarter of the way toward the center (c).

9 Fold this side again, meeting the first folded half in the center.

10 Fold the two halves together, ending with the open side facing you (d).

11 Using a sharp knife, cut the strip into even slices, approximately ⅜ inch to ½ inch (1 cm to 1.25 cm) thick (e).

12 Lay the slices cut side down on a parchment-lined sheet pan (f).

13 Place the sheet pan in the oven and bake until the bottoms of the palmiers are golden brown and caramelized, approximately 15 minutes.

14 Remove the pan from the oven. Working quickly, turn over each of the slices and return the pan to the oven.

15 Continue baking until the top is golden and caramelized, approximately 6 to 8 minutes.

16 Cool on the pan and store in an airtight container.

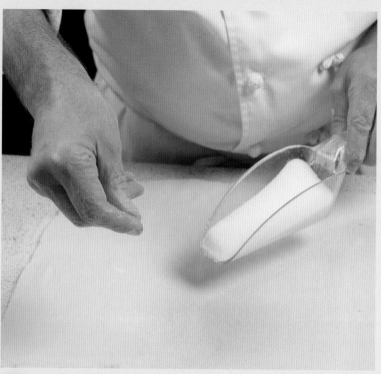

a Sprinkle sugar over the surface of the dough.

If desired, place the pastry dough in the freezer for 45 minutes before baking. Refrigerating the puff pastry dough for a minimum of one hour after forming the products allows the dough to relax, which will reduce shrinkage. However, palmiers are usually baked directly after fabrication because the sugar can liquefy in a humid refrigerator if they are refrigerated too long.

d Fold the two halves together.

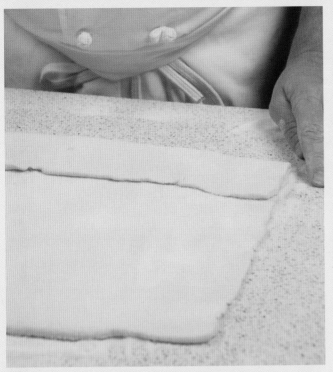

b Fold the edge of the dough one-quarter of the way toward the center.

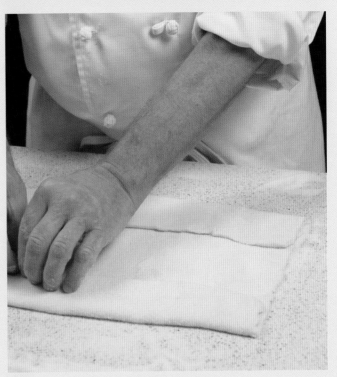

c Fold the opposite edge in the same way.

e Cut the strip into slices.

f Place the slices cut-side down on a prepared pan.

FRANZ ZIEGLER IS WIDELY REGARDED FOR HIS DELICATE AND INTRICATE WORK WITH MARZIPAN AND CHOCOLATE. SHAKING HANDS WITH HIM IS LIKE SHAKING HANDS WITH A CATCHER'S MITT. HE MAINTAINS AN ATHLETIC, RUGGED PHYSIQUE EQUAL TO HIS OUTSIZED, LARGER-THAN-LIFE PERSONALITY. HOW DOES A BIG MAN WITH BIG HANDS EXECUTE SUCH FINE WORK? DETERMINATION AND A COMPETITIVE NATURE THAT CAN BE TRACED TO HIS CHILDHOOD IN SWITZERLAND, WHERE HE WAS A SOCCER STAR IN HIS YOUTH. (IF IT HADN'T BEEN FOR KNEE DAMAGE, HE WOULD HAVE PURSUED THE SPORT TO HIGHER LEVELS.)

FRANZ ZIEGLER,
AUTHOR AND CONSULTANT

Since 2001, he has been the coach of the Swiss Pastry Team, stepping in to compete for an ill team member in 2004. He has served as the head judge of the National and World Pastry Team Championships.

Franz began working at an early age with his father in the family shop in the Swiss Alps. His fascination with learning and mastering the craft led him to other high-end shops in his homeland before he began his formal training. At the completion of his master's studies, he received the highest score in his class. He began working with a premier chocolate company as a technical advisor, traveling the world educating clientele on the proper use of chocolate. He continues that work today in addition to teaching, coaching, and consulting.

"Switzerland has a rich tradition. That is a plus, and it can be a minus when people are expected to uphold that tradition. We seem to do things slower, but better, in the long run."

Marzipan figurine

INTERVIEW WITH FRANZ ZIEGLER

HOW DID YOU BECOME ONE OF THE MOST RECOGNIZED PASTRY CHEFS IN SWITZERLAND, A COUNTRY WIDELY REGARDED AS ONE OF THE WORLD LEADERS IN THIS PROFESSION?

I grew up in a bakery/confectionary business, which my father owned. Waking up to the smell of fresh bread and grabbing a little bit of warm vanilla custard now and then made me realize what a beautiful, sensual profession being a pastry chef is. Then I did an apprenticeship away from home. Being home only for the weekends makes you grow up quickly and become tougher. After receiving my degree, I worked for my father for one year. That's when I attended further education classes with famous chefs in Switzerland, filling in the missing pieces of what I did not know. And there were many. I made a choice to work for high-end pastry shops in Switzerland in order to improve my skills. When I was 26, I immigrated to Australia. I planned to conquer that land and make an impression with my skills. I did not succeed; however, I got to know the land and the people. I returned to Switzerland and started working on my master's degree.

Felchlin (a large Swiss chocolate company) hired me as its executive pastry chef, and I spent five years traveling around the globe promoting its products. During that time I wrote my first book, *Magic Chocolate*. I was fortunate enough to meet a lot of very talented people all around the world, and exchanging and sharing ideas and techniques was a way of life. It was the foundation of what I have become today.

THE PASTRIES IN SWITZERLAND ARE SEEMINGLY TRADITIONAL AND MODERN AT THE SAME TIME. HOW IS THIS SO? DO YOU SEE A REVOLUTION, AS HAS HAPPENED IN OTHER EUROPEAN COUNTRIES?

I have observed the revolution everywhere. Maybe we started it, or maybe we are in the aftermath. Switzerland has a rich tradition. That is a plus, and it can be a minus when people are expected to uphold that tradition. We seem to do things slower, but better, in the long run. So we will see what comes out in the long run.

IN YOUR TRAVELS, DO YOU SEE A SWISS INFLUENCE IN OTHER COUNTRIES, WHETHER IN WORK, PRESENTATION, OR FLAVORS?

Hardly, except in chocolate. The Swiss invented many basic techniques and recipes in that field.

WHAT IS THE CONTEMPORARY MODEL FOR TEACHING AND TRAINING BEGINNING PASTRY CHEFS IN SWITZERLAND? APPRENTICESHIP? SCHOOL? A MIXTURE?

Apprenticeship is still there and will not go away. The world envies us for our system. It is the best in the world. No question.

YOU HAVE A STORIED HISTORY WITH COMPETITIONS AS A COMPETITOR AND JUDGE. WHAT KEEPS YOU GOING?

The top chefs are all alpha animals! Alpha animals want to know who the best alpha male out there is. That leads to competition. Of course, there is passion and all of that, but the ego is the driving force. That's the same with me. The higher you are up in the alpha male hierarchy, the calmer you become. Very philosophical, isn't it? Really, I love the exchange with my friends from all around the world. It is a true pleasure. And meeting them as a judge in competition is a joy. I have many close friends that I have made in that arena.

OVER THE YEARS, HOW HAS YOUR STYLE EVOLVED OR MATURED?

I become better every day, and that shows in my work. I work cleaner, and my final products are more refined. I like simple things. I guess every artist evolves into simplicity.

HOW DO YOU REMAIN MOTIVATED? HOW DO YOU REMAIN CURRENT?

As long as I have the energy and remain attached to the lifeline of the pastry world (competitions, fairs, magazines, etc.)—and the alpha male in me demands to prove something—I will remain up there. The moment I become overconfident and lazy, that will be the beginning of the end.

IS THERE ANYTHING YOU MISS ABOUT WORKING IN A SMALL SHOP?

Teamwork. And sometimes the physical work to get something done in a short time.

OTHER THAN BUTTER, FLOUR, SUGAR, EGGS, AND SALT, WHAT ARE THE FIRST TEN INGREDIENTS YOU WOULD SELECT FOR YOUR KITCHEN?

Chocolate, marzipan, vanilla, purées,

OTHER THAN AN OVEN, WHICH ITEMS ARE ESSENTIAL TO EQUIP YOUR KITCHEN?

A stand mixer with attachments, a hand blender, whisks, spatulas, an assortment of stainless steel bowls, modeling tools, and an airbrush.

WHAT WAS THE MOST DIFFICULT SKILL FOR YOU TO LEARN WHEN YOU WERE BEGINNING?

Combining speed and precision.

WHAT IS THE FIRST THING YOU TEACH A NEW TEAM MEMBER OR STUDENT?

Reliability, teamwork, and dedication.

WHAT ARE THE GUIDING PRINCIPLES/RULES OF YOUR KITCHEN?

Reliability, teamwork, and dedication.

WHICH GIVES YOU MORE PLEASURE? MAKING PASTRY OR EATING PASTRY?

I am simple guy: eating!

WHAT IS YOUR GREATEST STRENGTH? WHAT IS YOUR BIGGEST WEAKNESS?

The whole Franz Ziegler package (skills, personality, smarts, knowing what the business wants). My biggest weakness is the daily temptations of sweets.

WHAT ARE YOUR GOALS FOR THE FUTURE?

Writing more books, passing on my knowledge, being a good mentor and teacher, and continuing to learn and keep my curiosity alive.

WORDS TO LIVE BY?

Take your chances!

Yield: 1 pound, 6.3 ounces (632 g), or enough dough for two 4-inch (10 cm) Engadine Nuss Tortes, one 9-inch (23 cm) Engadine Nuss Torte, or two 9-inch (23 cm) fruit tarts

Preparation time: active time 40 minutes; total time, 2 hours 40 minutes

Equipment needed: Pastry scraper, circle cutter (sized to match the tart pan), rolling pin, tart pan(s), pastry brush, fork

TART CRUST/ ENGADINE NUSS TORTE
BY FRANZ ZIEGLER

The engadine nuss torte is one of the most famous pastries (not including chocolate) from Switzerland. It combines a tender, slightly flaky pastry with chewy, nutty caramel. Walnuts are traditionally used; however, this version incorporates slivered almonds to fill in the natural gaps formed when only walnuts are used. One of the remarkable qualities of the engadine nuss torte is its shelf life. It keeps for weeks when stored tightly covered at room temperature. It is sturdy enough to ship around the world; there are several companies in Switzerland that do so. Serve this rich torte in thin slivers.

INGREDIENTS

	U.S. Imperial Weight	Metric Weight	Volume
Flour	10.6 oz	300 g	1¾ cups
Confectioners' sugar	1.1 oz	30 g	¼ cup
Salt	.07 oz	2 g	¼ teaspoon
Unsalted butter*	5.3 oz	150 g	11 tablespoons
Egg, lightly beaten			3 eggs
Lemon juice			From half a lemon
Engadine Nuss Torte Filling (see recipe following)			1 recipe
Whole egg			1 egg

Recipe note: Use cold, European-style butter (minimum 82% fat content).

PROCEDURE (see photos, pages 78–83)

1 Combine the flour, confectioners' sugar, and salt. Make into a mound on a flat work surface.

2 Cut the cold butter into cubes and add it to the dry ingredients.

3 Using a pastry scraper, begin chopping the butter into the flour until the butter is in small particles and the mixture resembles coarse cornmeal (a).

4 Make a well in the mixture. Add the lightly beaten egg and lemon juice.

5 Using your fingertips, gradually work the flour/butter mixture into the liquid using a plastic scraper to assist, if necessary.

6 Form the dough into a rough ball (b). Use the heel of your hand to smear the dough across the work surface. Gather the dough into a ball and repeat the smearing process with the heel of your hand.

7 Form the dough into a tight ball, then wrap in plastic (c) and press to form a disc (d).

8 Refrigerate for a minimum of 2 hours.

9 Preheat oven to 350°F (180°C or gas mark 4).

10 Remove the dough from the refrigerator and place it on a lightly floured work surface.

11 Using a rolling pin, roll the dough in different directions to create a disc that is approximately 3 inches (7.5 cm) larger than the tart pan. Rotate the dough 90° several times throughout the process and dust the work surface with more flour, if necessary.

12 Roll the dough to a thickness of ¼ inch (0.6 cm). With the tines of a fork, pierce (dock) the dough and return to the refrigerator for a minimum of 30 minutes to minimize shrinkage.

13 Use a circle cutter to cut two discs of dough for each of the tart pan(s) you are using.

14 Line the bottom(s) of the pan(s) with one circle of dough each (e). Place the dough circles for the top of the torte in the refrigerator.

15 Place the tart pans in the oven and bake until half baked, approximately 8 to 10 minutes; the dough will be pale and slightly dry. Remove from the oven.

16 Using the dough trimmings, form a ½-inch (1.3 cm) cylinder long enough to wrap around the interior edge of the tart pan (f).

17 Lightly moisten the edge of the dough circle in the tart pan with water (g).

18 Press the cylinder into the fluted sides of the tart pan, sealing it to the bottom circle of dough (h).

19 Remove the filling (see recipe following) from the refrigerator.

20 Spray a work surface with nonstick cooking spray.

21 Place the filling on the sprayed work surface and form a ball. Flatten the ball and press it out until it is nearly the size of the tart pan.

22 Place the filling on top of the half-baked crust and press it evenly to the edges of the pan (i).

23 Lightly moisten the top edge of the dough with water (j).

24 Remove the dough circle(s) from the refrigerator and slide it into position on top of the filling (k).

25 Press the edges of the circle into the moistened dough around the edge of the pan, encasing the filling.

26 Lightly beat the remaining egg. Brush the surface of the dough with beaten egg (l).

27 Using the tines of a fork, apply medium pressure to make a decorative pattern in the torte top (m).

28 Puncture the surface of the dough in a few places to allow steam to escape.

29 Bake until golden brown, approximately 30 to 35 minutes.

30 Remove from the oven and place on a cooling rack.

a Note the texture of the flour mixture.

b Form the dough into a rough ball.

Rolling the dough out in several directions prevents the dough from sticking and will minimize the possibility of elasticity (shrinkage in the dough)—if the dough is continuously rolled in the same direction, the gluten could develop in one direction, which causes the dough to shrink during baking.

e Line the bottom of the tart pan with a dough circle.

f Roll the dough trimmings into a long cylinder.

c Wrap the dough in plastic.

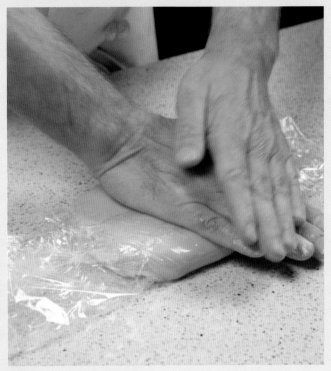

d Press the dough into a disc.

g Moisten the edges of the dough.

h Press the cylinder into the sides of the tart pan.

i The filled tart pan.

(continued)

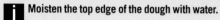

j Moisten the top edge of the dough with water.

k Slide another dough circle on top of the filling.

Partially baking the base of the tart prior to filling it ensures that it will be fully baked when the caramel and tart top have baked. The caramel liquefies a bit before it firms after baking.

Rolling the dough into a cylinder to flute the sides is an innovative solution to an often troublesome task, especially in a warm kitchen.

l Brush the top of the torte with beaten egg.

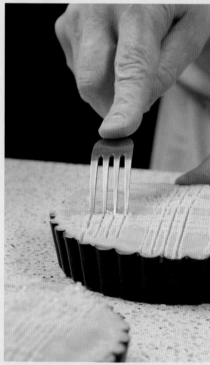

m Use a fork to make a decorative pattern in the torte top.

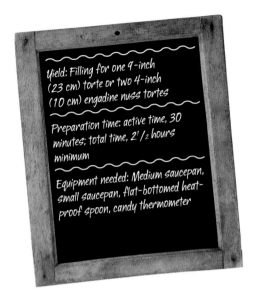

ENGADINE NUSS TORTE FILLING
BY FRANZ ZIEGLER

The torte filling will keep in the refrigerator for up to one month. It has a high percentage of sugar and little to no water activity, so no harmful bacteria can gain a foothold.

INGREDIENTS

	U.S. Imperial Weight	Metric Weight	Volume
Walnut halves	7.7 oz	218 g	2½ cups
Slivered almonds	1.6 oz	44 g	½ cup
Heavy cream			¼ cup
Water			¼ cup minus 1 teaspoon
Honey			1 tablespoon
Vanilla bean			¼ bean
Unsalted butter, softened*	0.9 oz	26.3 g	2 tablespoons
Glucose	0.4 oz	11.3 g	1 teaspoon
Granulated sugar	8.8 oz	250 g	1¼ cup

Recipe note: Use European-style butter (minimum 82% fat content).

PROCEDURE

1 Preheat oven to 350°F (180°C or gas mark 4).

2 Combine the walnuts and almonds on a sheet pan and toast lightly in the oven, approximately 10 to 12 minutes (a). After the nuts are toasted, open the oven door and leave them in the oven to remain warm.

3 Place the heavy cream, water, honey, vanilla bean, and butter in a heavy-bottomed pot. Keep warm over medium heat, keeping the temperature below the boiling point.

4 Place the glucose in a separate heavy-bottomed pot with tall, steep sides and place over medium heat.

5 Cook until the glucose liquefies, then add a small amount of the sugar (b). Cook until the sugar is caramelized (c).

6 Continue adding sugar gradually until all of the sugar has been added and it is caramelized (d).

7 With caution, gradually add the warmed cream mixture to the caramel. The disparity between the two temperatures will cause rapid, intense boiling in the pot (e). Use a long-handled spoon or spatula to stir.

8 When the cream mixture has been fully incorporated, cook the contents of the pot to a temperature of 232°F (111°C) (f).

9 Add the warmed nuts and stir to combine (g).

10 Pour the caramel—nut mixture into a container and refrigerate until needed.

Incorporating glucose into the caramel adds acidity, which inhibits sugar crystallization. It also contributes to the pliability and shine of the caramel. When you don't use glucose in cooking sugar, you must meticulously wash the sides of the pot with a wet pastry brush throughout the process to prevent crystallization. It's a simple solution to something that could easily lead to failure.

a Toast the walnuts and almonds in the oven.

e Carefully add the cream mixture to the caramelized sugar mixture.

b Add a little of the sugar at a time to the glucose.

c Cook until the sugar mixture caramelizes.

d Gradually add the remaining sugar, cooking until caramelized.

f Use a thermometer to check the temperature of the liquid.

g Stir the warmed nuts into the caramel.

THE GOOD SON. THAT'S HOW THADDEUS DESCRIBES HIS FORMATIVE YEARS, FIRST IN CALIFORNIA AND LATER IN IDAHO. THE THIRD CHILD OF SIX SIBLINGS, HE WAS THE FIRST ONE TO HELP IN THE GARDEN, TO COOK AND CLEAN IN THE KITCHEN, OR TO ASSIST WITH OTHER CHORES. HE WAS THE "GOODIE-GOODIE" AT HOME AND AT SCHOOL, WHERE HIS WORK WAS IN THE TOP PERCENTILE. THIS BEHAVIOR REFLECTS THE TRAITS SEEMINGLY INHERENT IN ALL GREAT PASTRY CHEFS: THE ABILITY TO WORK LONG HOURS, OR-GANIZATION, COOPERATION, TEAMWORK, THE DESIRE TO PLEASE OTHERS, AND THE DETERMINATION TO SUCCEED.

THADDEUS DUBOIS,
FORMER WHITE HOUSE EXECUTIVE PASTRY CHEF, PASTRY CHEF AT THE BORGATA HOTEL & CASINO AND CULINARY MENTOR

INTERVIEW WITH THADDEUS DUBOIS

WAS THERE A DEFINING MOMENT WHEN YOU KNEW THAT BAKING AND PASTRY WAS MORE THAN A LOVE AND WOULD BE YOUR LIFE'S WORK?

I was always interested in four careers: music, pastry arts, horticulture, and meteorology. I received two BAs in music; however, during these studies I became more interested in pastry and thought it would make a better career.

WHAT ARE THE DIFFERENCES AND SIMILARITIES BETWEEN A CAREER IN MUSIC AND A CAREER IN PASTRY?

There are many similarities in the careers. Both require thousands of hours of practice perfecting coordination and precision of the hands. They both require strength and

HOW WOULD YOU DESCRIBE A PASTRY CHEF TO SOMEONE WHO HAD NEVER HEARD OF ONE?

A pastry chef is someone who is completely dedicated to his or her craft—passionate to the point of being crazy—and is the neighbor who always brings dessert to get-togethers.

YOUR ASCENT TO THE TOP LEVEL OF YOUR CRAFT WAS RAPID. HOW DO YOU EXPLAIN THAT?

I decided that if I were going to do this as a career that I wanted to move up quickly, so I worked incredibly long hours with many great pastry chefs, did lots of competitions, read tons of books, and poured my entire life into it, like jumping head-first into a deep pool.

WHAT ROLE DID MENTORING

HOW WOULD YOU DEFINE YOUR STYLE?

My style relies on using ingredients that are appropriate to the season, my location, and my ability to combine flavors to suit the situation. I like to use fresh, local ingredients that fit the criteria for the event, restaurant, or show. My style depends on what Mother Earth lays at my feet. I just hope she is happy after I have worked with her creations.

OTHER THAN BUTTER, FLOUR, SUGAR, EGGS, AND SALT, WHAT ARE THE FIRST TEN INGREDIENTS YOU WOULD SELECT FOR YOUR KITCHEN?

Dark chocolate, almonds, lemons, hazelnuts, oranges, cinnamon, tapioca, heavy cream, apples, and agar-agar.

OTHER THAN AN OVEN, WHICH ITEMS ARE ESSENTIAL FOR EQUIPPING YOUR HOME KITCHEN?

A stand mixer with a minimum bowl capacity of 5 quarts (4.7 L), pastry bags and tips, parchment paper, nonstick mats, commercial quality half sheet pans, a hand whip,

Rock n' roll wedding cake

"The traits seemingly inherent in all great pastry chefs: the ability to work long hours, organization, cooperation, teamwork, the desire to please others, and the determination to succeed."

...ound myself with other chefs, colleagues, and young, inspired souls who are striving to make a career in pastry. This is a people business, after all.

WHAT WAS THE MOST DIFFICULT SKILL FOR YOU TO LEARN WHEN YOU WERE BEGINNING?

Understanding the baking process. Knowing when the different products are done to form maximum flavor. When I was learning, I would overbake or underbake almost everything. My chef at the time asked why I had pulled cookies that were clearly not done baking. I replied that they were firm and done. He pointed to the pale edges and commented that they were not properly caramelized and would be lacking in flavor. Learning when something is done and when something is *really* done is an acquired skill. It seems that many beginners pull products from the oven based on a fear of overbaking. I tell my team that timers are

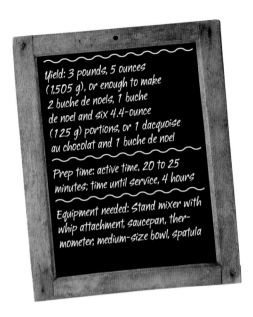

Yield: 3 pounds, 5 ounces (1,505 g), or enough to make 2 buche de noels, 1 buche de noel and six 4.4-ounce (125 g) portions, or 1 dacquoise au chocolat and 1 buche de noel

Prep time: active time, 20 to 25 minutes; time until service, 4 hours

Equipment needed: Stand mixer with whip attachment, saucepan, thermometer, medium-size bowl, spatula

CHOCOLATE MOUSSE
BY THADDEUS DUBOIS

Pastry chef Thaddeus Dubois's chocolate mousse uses a classic *pâte à bombe* preparation, a technique that provides stability to all mousses and adds richness, especially to chocolate mousse.

INGREDIENTS

	U.S. Imperial Weight	Metric Weight	Volume
Dark chocolate*	14 oz	400 g	
Unsweetened chocolate	1 oz	30 g	
Heavy cream	1 lb, 5 oz	600 g	2½ cups
Egg yolk	6 oz	175 g	3½ yolks
Whole egg	2.5 oz	75 g	1½ eggs
Water	2.5 oz	75 g	⅓ cup
Granulated sugar	5.3 oz	150 g	¾ cup

Recipe notes: Eggs should be at room temperature.

*Couverature quality 55–64%

PROCEDURE

1 Combine the dark and unsweetened chocolate in a heatproof bowl and place over a pot of simmering water to melt. After the chocolate has melted, maintain a temperature of 100°F (37°C).

2 In the bowl of a stand mixer fitted with the whip attachment or with a handheld whisk, whip the heavy cream to soft peaks (a). Refrigerate.

3 Place the egg yolks and eggs in the bowl of a stand mixer fitted with the whip attachment. Whip the egg yolks and eggs on medium speed.

4 Stir the water and sugar together in a small saucepan. Cook over medium heat until the mixture reaches 180°F (82°C) and the sugar is completely dissolved.

5 Reduce the mixing speed to low and slowly pour the sugar syrup into the egg mixture, avoiding the sides of the bowl and the whip attachment (b).

6 After the syrup has been added, increase the mixing speed to medium-high.

7 Continue whipping until the mixture is pale yellow, the outside of the mixing bowl is cool, and the mixture forms a ribbon (when the whip is lifted out of the mixture, the mixture falls on the surface of the mixture and does not sink into the mixture). This is your *pâte à bombe* (c).

8 Add the melted chocolate to the *pâte à bombe*. Mix on medium speed to incorporate (d).

9 When the chocolate is fully incorporated, fold one-third of the whipped cream into the chocolate mixture. This will lighten the mixture so the remaining cream will not deflate when folded into the mixture. Fold in the remaining cream (e).

10 Spoon or ladle into cups, glasses, or molds (f), or leave in the mixing bowl and portion later.

11 Cover and refrigerate the mousse until it is ready to serve.

Thaddeus prefers to cook the syrup to 180°F (82°C) instead of 250°F (121°C), as has been traditionally suggested; less because "it increases the moisture level and allows all the syrup to flow from the pan into the whipping egg mixture. It is advantageous to cook it like this if the mousse is to be served in either an edible or inedible container in that the mousse can be served slightly softer, creating a more luxurious mouthfeel.

a Whip the cream to soft peaks.

d Add the melted chocolate to the egg and sugar mixture.

b Pour the sugar into the eggs while mixing.

c Note the consistency of the whipped egg and sugar mixture. This is your pâte à bombe.

e Fold the whipped cream into the chocolate mixture.

f Spoon the chocolate mousse into serving glasses.

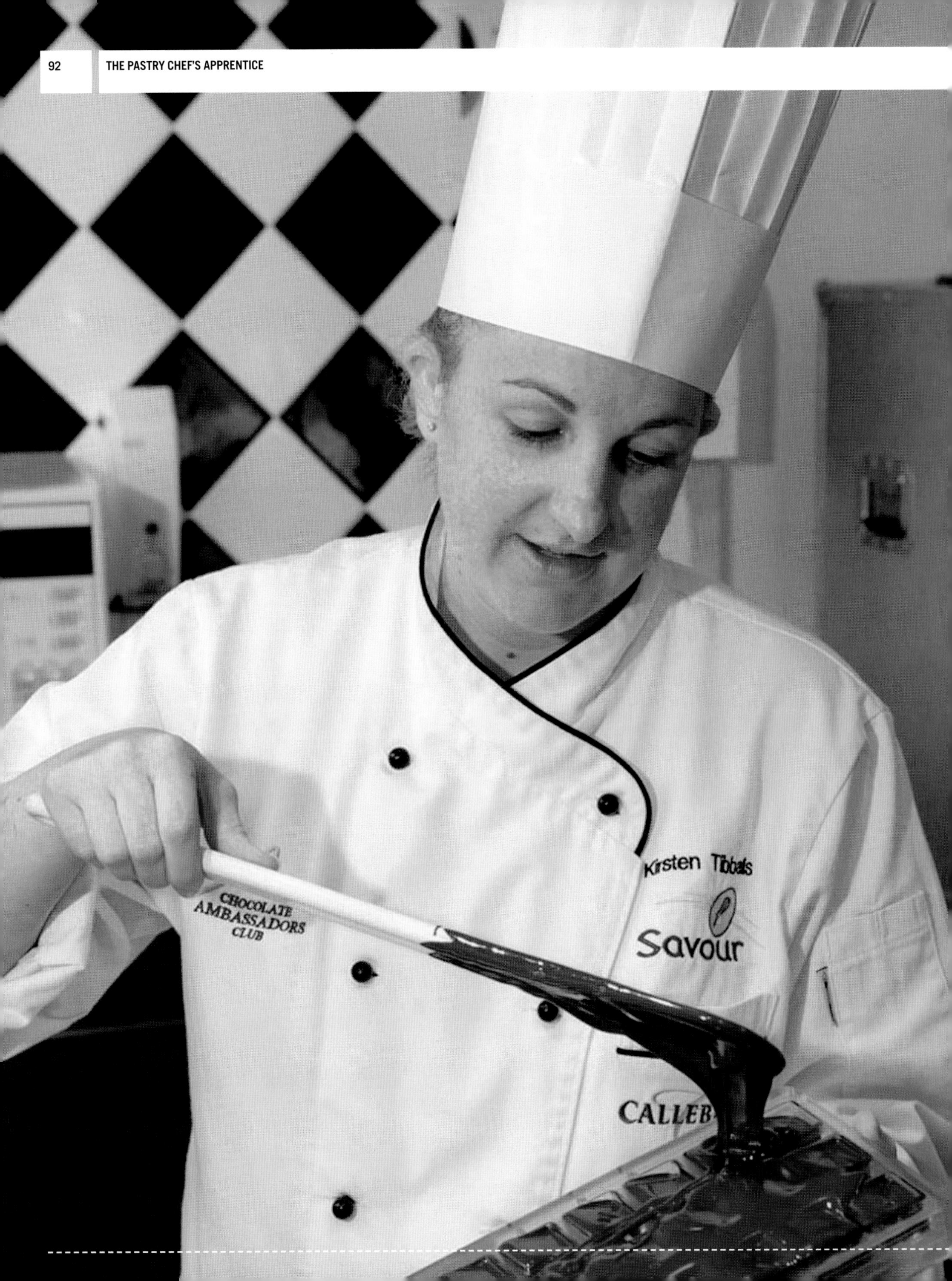
CHOCOLATE
AMBASSADORS
CLUB
Kirsten Tibbals
Savour

ONE OF THE MOST POPULAR—AND HIGHLY REGARDED—BAKING AND PASTRY PERSONALITIES IN AUSTRALIA IS KIRSTEN TIBBALLS. SHE BEGAN COOKING AT HOME WITH HER MOTHER, AND WHEN SHE WAS FIFTEEN YEARS OLD, SHE BEGAN A FIVE-YEAR APPRENTICESHIP, DURING WHICH SHE WON THE NATIONAL BAKE SKILLS COMPETITION. SHE CONTINUED HER STUDIES IN AUSTRALIA AND IN EUROPE.

KIRSTEN TIBBALLS,
FOUNDER OF SAVOUR CHOCOLATE AND
PATISSERIE SCHOOL IN MELBOURNE

World record pastry creation of largest chocolate flower display

HOW WOULD YOU DESCRIBE YOUR BAKING AND PASTRY STYLE?

I love the principles of classic French patisserie, but I like to evolve that into my own product with a modern flair. I like using different textures both for tasting and for finishing.

HOW HAS YOUR STYLE EVOLVED OVER TIME?

My style has been influenced by many of the pastry chefs I have worked with both in Australia and Europe. When I first started over twenty years ago, the style of cakes were quite often made with a layered sponge filled with buttercream, custard, or creams, then masked in buttercream to create a perfect clean base for the ganache coating. This style of cake has morphed into a sleek mousse-style cake with crunchy bases, textured inserts, light mousse, shiny glazes, and very minimalistic garnishes. Food is like fashion that changes style regularly.

INTERVIEW WITH KIRSTEN TIBBALLS

WHICH GIVES YOU THE MOST PLEASURE: EATING PASTRIES AND

WHAT ARE SOME OF THE TYPICAL BAKED GOODS AND PASTRIES MADE IN AUSTRALIAN HOMES?

We have a very multicultural population in Australia, and this is reflected in what is created at home. Muffins, cupcakes, Pavalova, and scones would be some common typically Australian baked goods made at home.

OTHER THAN BUTTER, FLOUR, SUGAR, EGGS, AND SALT, WHAT ARE THE FIRST TEN INGREDIENTS YOU WOULD SELECT FOR YOUR KITCHEN?

Cacao Barry Alto El Sol plantation couverture, Boiron passion fruit purée, hazelnut praline paste, mountain pepper, fresh cream, cream of tartar, almond meal, cocoa powder 22 to 24 percent, gelatin, and vanilla.

OTHER THAN AN OVEN, WHICH ITEMS ARE ESSENTIAL TO EQUIP YOUR HOME KITCHEN?

A microplane grater, a stick blender, good quality knives, a silicone baking mat, and a food processor.

WHAT WAS THE MOST DIFFICULT SKILL FOR YOU TO LEARN WHEN YOU WERE BEGINNING?

For me, the most difficult skill to learn was neat and creative writing with chocolate and also laminating puff pastry. Lots of practice has paid off.

WHAT IS YOUR THOUGHT PROCESS WHEN WRITING A PASTRY MENU?

I like to use seasonal and local produce where I can and make sure I balance flavors and textures. I believe the garnish should always complement the product and be completely edible.

WHAT ARE THE GUIDING PRINCIPLES/RULES OF YOUR KITCHEN?

I like my kitchen to be extremely clean at all times. I like everyone to share concepts and ideas. The student is always the most important person in the room. They also need to understand that you never stop learning so to keep an open mind.

WHAT IS YOUR GREATEST STRENGTH? WHAT IS YOUR BIGGEST WEAKNESS?

I think my number one strength is my passion and drive to improve what I create on a daily basis, and to pass that knowledge on to those that I teach. Also, my love of all things chocolate. My biggest weakness is wanting to spend time with my family and being torn between my two loves.

HOW DO YOU STAY MOTIVATED?

My work colleague, Paul Kennedy, keeps me motivated. He is an extremely talented pastry chef, and we push each other to improve what we do. I also travel extensively every year to view international pastry competitions, which keeps me abreast of what is new and innovative.

WORDS TO LIVE BY?

"When you think you have learned all there is to learn, it is time to retire."

Coco loco oval petit gateaux

"When you think you have learned all there is to learn, it is time to retire."

Yield: 4 pounds, 2 ounces (1,874 g), or enough for two 9-inch (23 cm) Black Forest tortes

Prep time: 30 minutes

Equipment needed: 4-quart (3.8 L) saucepan, digital thermometer, stand mixer fitted with whip attachment

ITALIAN BUTTERCREAM
BY KIRSTEN TIBBALLS

INGREDIENTS

	U.S. Imperial Weight	Metric Weight	Volume
Granulated sugar	1 lb, 5.2 oz	600 g	3 cups minus 2 tablespoons + 1 teaspoon
Water			½ cup + 2 tablespoons
Egg white			11 egg whites
Unsalted butter*	1 lb, 10.2 oz	743 g	3¼ cups
Salt	0.04 oz	1 g	⅛ teaspoon
Vanilla extract			1 teaspoon

Recipe note: Use European-style butter (minimum 82% fat content).

Italian buttercream is a lighter alternative to French and American buttercreams. Pastry chefs like it because it uses all the egg whites left over from pastries that require an abundance of egg yolks. Pouring the hot sugar syrup into the whipping egg white cooks it to a safe temperature. Stored in an airtight container, Italian buttercream keeps for days in the refrigerator and is useful for many projects. To use, remove it from the refrigerator and leave at room temperature until it is soft and spreadable. Transfer the buttercream to the bowl of a stand mixer fitted with the paddle attachment. Mix on medium-slow speed until the buttercream is smooth and light. In a hurry? Melt a small amount of the cold buttercream in the bowl of a stand mixer (use a torch or stove flame). Begin mixing on medium speed, adding the remaining cold buttercream in increments until it is fully incorporated and the mixture is smooth and creamy.

PROCEDURE

1 In a heavy-bottomed pot, stir the sugar into the water. Place the pot over medium-high heat. Place the probe of a digital thermometer in the pot.

2 While the sugar mixture cooks, begin whipping the egg whites on medium speed in the bowl of a stand mixer fitted with the whip attachment (a).

3 Do not stir the sugar syrup while it cooks; wash the sides of the pot with a wet brush to prevent crystallization (b). Boil the syrup until it reaches 250°F (120°C) (c). Remove the pot from the stove.

4 Lower the mixer speed to medium-low and pour the syrup slowly into the egg whites in between the whip and the side of the bowl (d).

5 After all the syrup has been incorporated, resume mixing on medium speed and whip until the meringue is cool.

6 Cream the butter in a mixing bowl to soften it, or pound it with a rolling pin until it's pliable. Add the butter gradually to the cooled meringue.

7 Add the salt and vanilla after half of the butter has been incorporated.

8 Continue whipping until all ingredients are combined and the buttercream is smooth, light, and creamy.

9 Use directly or store in the refrigerator until needed. To use refrigerated buttercream, melt a small portion over simmering water and add it to the cold buttercream in the bowl of a stand mixer fitted with the paddle attachment. Whip smooth.

VARIATIONS:

1 For chocolate buttercream, add 8.8 ounces (250 g) melted chocolate along with the salt and vanilla (e).

2 For mocha buttercream, make a paste with hot water and espresso-grind instant coffee and add to the chocolate buttercream to taste, approximately 2 ounces (57 g), along with the salt and vanilla.

a Beat the egg whites until they form soft peaks.

b Wash down the sides of the pot to prevent sugar crystals from forming.

(continued)

c Check the temperature of the sugar syrup.

d Slowly pour the syrup into the whipped egg whites.

e The finished buttercream

Salt in buttercream? In small amounts, salt balances the flavors of butter and vanilla and enhances the sweetness without the use of more sugar. It also mitigates the greasiness some people perceive when eating buttercream.

With its light texture, Italian buttercream is a flavor chameleon. Simply adding melted bittersweet chocolate, coffee extract, or liqueur to buttercream can flavor it to suit any occasion.

KNOWN AS MUCH FOR HIS SENSE OF HUMOR AS HE IS FOR HIS CONTRIBUTIONS TO THE PROFESSION AND TO THE INDUSTRY, ROBERT HAS A METHODICAL, SCIENTIFIC APPROACH TO PASTRY MAKING. HE WAS AWARDED DEGREES IN BAKING AND IN FOOD SCIENCE BY THE HIGHBURY TECHNICAL COLLEGE IN PORTSMOUTH, ENGLAND, BEFORE RECEIVING HIS BACHELOR'S DEGREE IN HOTEL AND RESTAURANT MANAGEMENT FROM FLORIDA INTERNATIONAL UNIVERSITY.

ROBERT ELLINGER,
OWNER OF BAKED TO PERFECTION, FOUNDER OF THE GUILD OF BAKING AND PASTRY ARTS, AND INTERNATIONAL PASTRY COMPETITION JUDGE

After graduation, he relocated to New York City, where he spent time as the pastry chef at the Metropolitan Opera, the United Nations, the Water Club, and the Garden City Hotel. Desiring more control over his life and time spent with his family, Robert moved to Port Washington, New York, in 1986 to open his dream shop, Baked to Perfection. In addition to managing the bakery, Robert travels extensively as a business partner of Ice Cream University, training clients in the production of ice cream.

In the ensuing years, *Pastry Art & Design* magazine acknowledged him as one of the Top Ten Pastry Chefs in 2002 and again in 2009, the same year he was presented with the Medal of the French Government by Andre Soltner. In 2010, he served as the head judge at the World Team Pastry Championships.

"I believe that the savory side
and the pastry side need to
work together to help and
teach each other."

Amoretti

201

INTERVIEW WITH ROBERT ELLINGER

YOU HAVE DEGREES IN FOOD SCIENCE, PASTRY SCIENCE, AND MANAGEMENT. WOULD YOU SAY YOU ARE A PASTRY CHEF WHO IS A SCIENTIST OR A SCIENTIST WHO IS A PASTRY CHEF?

I have formal management and culinary training in the United States and in Europe. I also had apprenticeships, which consisted of management and pastry training. In terms of being a scientist or a pastry chef, my opinion is that they go hand in hand. I believe that to be a cutting-edge pastry chef, one really needs to know every ingredient that goes into a recipe and how those ingredients work together. This way, there are no limits to one's creativity.

WHY SHOULD SOMEONE BECOME A PASTRY CHEF?

One word: passion. Without passion, it's just a job with long hours, weekends, and holidays, but if you have passion and love for the pastry arts, you will be challenged (in a good way) every day. If you're creative, inquisitive, and driven, this is a great profession to be in.

HOW DID YOU DEVELOP YOUR PASTRY PALATE AND SENSIBILITY?

I developed a strategy that I have used my entire pastry career. The pH level of the human body is 7. Butter, chocolate, eggs, flour, and sugar all have pH levels set closely around 7. I believe that the closer the pH level of a product is to 7, the more immediately acceptable it will be to the customer. When I deviate and go lower on the pH scale, I find that fewer people will like the product right away. They might enjoy it over time, but it is initially more of a shock to the system because the body's pH is so much higher. I have experimented with this theory on a daily basis [for twenty-five years], and I find this to be true.

WITH YOUR NEWLY FOUNDED GUILD OF BAKING AND PASTRY ARTS [IN THE UNITED STATES], WHAT DO YOU HOPE TO ACHIEVE?

I founded the Guild of Baking and Pastry Arts for many reasons. One, the pastry chefs and bakers need a home. Like any profession, we need a place where we can network, share ideas, and be passionate about something that is common ground. So often, pastry chefs and bakers are combined with the savory side of the business. I believe that the savory side and the pastry side need to work together to help and teach each other. Now that culinary schools have specific pastry and baking programs, it's natural that there is a specific pastry and baking guild. My hope is that [all major cities] will have a chapter of the Guild of Baking and Pastry Arts so that each local chapter will have its own networking, education, and scholarship programs.

OTHER THAN BUTTER, FLOUR, SUGAR, EGGS, AND SALT, WHAT ARE THE FIRST TEN INGREDIENTS YOU WOULD SELECT FOR YOUR KITCHEN?

Maltitol, herbs, dried and fresh fruit, nuts, cinnamon, chocolate, invert syrups, vanilla, cheeses, and cream.

OTHER THAN AN OVEN, WHICH ITEMS ARE ESSENTIAL TO EQUIP YOUR HOME KITCHEN?

A stand mixer, food processor, stick blender, stainless steel saucepan, heat-resistant spatula, half sheet pan (allows for more consistent baking), and parchment paper.

WHICH OF YOUR JOBS BEFORE OPENING YOUR OWN SHOP WAS THE MOST INTERESTING AND/OR CHALLENGING?

Definitely working as the executive pastry chef at the United Nations. To this day, I refer back to the experiences dealing with all the different requirements of all the ambassadors from around the world. To call it "challenging" is an understatement.

WHAT WAS THE MOST DIFFICULT SKILL FOR YOU TO LEARN WHEN YOU WERE BEGINNING?

For me, it was cake decorating. In order for me to be proficient at it, I could not be under stress or under time constraints.

DOES CAKE DECORATING STILL TROUBLE YOU?

Yes, cake decorating can still trouble me, because stress stifles my creativity, and at the bakery there are always time constraints and stress. I would rather stop what I'm doing until the stress level wanes before I can resume what I'm doing.

WHAT IS YOUR THOUGHT PROCESS WHEN WRITING A PASTRY MENU?

I use the five Cs as my guide: cheese, coffee, citrus, chocolate, and caramel. From these basic concepts, I can elaborate tremendously. I think the most important thing a pastry chef should remember is that everyone has different likes and dislikes, and you need to find a middle ground. As a pastry chef, you could believe something to be the best dessert ever created, but the customer might feel otherwise.

WHAT IS THE FIRST THING YOU TELL A NEW TEAM MEMBER OR STUDENT?

"Put your hands up." I use a hands-on technique to demonstrate the pace of the bakery and how to survive. I engage the employee in a double high-five or a pattycake type of gesture with a constant rhythm. I explain that the bakery is in constant motion: it will never stop coming at you, so if you don't engage with the same intensity, you'll fall behind and get overloaded. By constantly moving, you can stay on track or even get ahead.

WHAT ARE THE GUIDING PRINCIPLES/RULES OF YOUR KITCHEN?

I strive for T.O.P.S.: Think, Organize, Precision, Speed. I try to instill this concept in my staff. The staff members who don't have a high level of passion have a much more difficult time with this. They might be talented at what they do, but if they don't have the heart, it becomes just a job for them. However, I always encourage them to challenge themselves.

IF YOU WERE FORCED TO CHOOSE BETWEEN EATING PASTRY AND MAKING PASTRY FOR THE REST OF YOUR LIFE, WHICH WOULD IT BE?

I would have to say making pastry; I love the pastry arts. There is so much to learn and experiment with. In a way, I've already adopted this into my life: otherwise how would I keep my gorgeous figure?

WHAT IS YOUR GREATEST STRENGTH?

Creativity is definitely my greatest strength. I come up with ideas any time of day. Some of my best ideas wake me up at night. I feel that there is no end to what can be created within the pastry arts.

YOU'RE INVITED TO SOMEONE'S HOME FOR DINNER. WHICH PRODUCT FROM YOUR SHOP DO YOU TAKE?

I would take the Ellinger dream, my favorite dessert. It is made up of caramel-almond wafers with pure vanilla gelato and dipped in dark chocolate on two edges. Since this dessert is one of my original creations, it becomes a much more personal gift.

WORDS TO LIVE BY?

Give me Danish or give me death!

Yield: 1 pound, 12 ounces (790 g), or enough to fill two 9 x 1-inch (23 x 2.5 cm) fruit tarts or 36 petit éclairs

Preparation time: active time, 15 minutes; time until use, 2 hours

Equipment needed: One 4- to 5-quart (3.8 to 4.7 L) saucepan, 2 medium mixing bowls, large bowl for ice bath, stiff wire whisk

PASTRY CREAM
BY ROBERT ELLINGER

Seldom eaten alone, pastry cream highlights and elevates other components. It is one of the first items a pastry cook learns to make on the path to becoming a pastry chef, and its cooking is a daily ritual in busy pastry kitchens. It is used as a baked filling in tarts, Parisian flan, and Danishes. It is elevated to as starring role in Napoleons, éclairs, and fruit tarts.

INGREDIENTS

	U.S. Imperial Weight	Metric Weight	Volume
Whole milk	1 lb, 1.6 oz	500 g	2 cups + 2 tablespoons
Vanilla bean	½ bean	½ bean	½ bean
Cornstarch	1.3 oz	38 g	¼ cup
Granulated sugar	4.4 oz	126 g	¼ cup + 1 tablespoon
Egg yolk	3.3 oz	93 g	2 yolks
Unsalted butter, softened*	1.2 oz	33 g	1½ tablespoons

Recipe note: Use European-style butter (minimum 82% fat content).

PROCEDURE

1 In a heavy-bottomed, nonreactive pot, heat the milk, the vanilla bean pod, and its scrapings until bubbles begin to form around the edge of the pot (a). Set aside for 30 minutes, allowing the vanilla to infuse the milk.

2 In a medium bowl, combine the cornstarch and 2.2 ounces (63 g) of sugar. Add the egg yolk and use a whisk to make a smooth paste (b).

3 Stir the remaining 2.2 ounces (63 g) of sugar into the infused vanilla/milk. Return the pot to the stove and bring to a boil.

4 When the mixture begins to boil, remove the pot from the stove. Slowly pour one-third of the boiling mixture into the yolk/starch/sugar paste, whisking briskly. This is known as tempering (c).

5 Quickly stir the tempered mixture into the remaining milk mixture in the pot and return to medium-high heat (d).

6 Stirring vigorously and constantly with a stiff wire whisk, cook until the mixture is bubbling, approximately 2 or 3 minutes.

7 Remove from the stove and pour into a shallow container (e). Alternatively, pour the pastry cream into a clean bowl, then place the bowl in a larger bowl of ice water and stir periodically to cool.

8 When the pastry cream is 86–88°F (30–31°C), remove it from the ice bath and briskly whisk in the softened butter (f).

9 To prevent a skin from forming, place plastic wrap or parchment paper on the surface of the pastry cream and refrigerate until cool.

10 When cool, transfer the pastry cream to a covered, airtight container. Use within three days. Before using, place the pastry cream in a bowl and whisk smooth.

Tempering equalizes the temperatures of the two components. Pouring cold eggs into the heated milk/sugar mixture would result in particles of coagulated egg. In addition, the pastry cream would not be as thick. Cornstarch is the primary thickening agent in pastry cream; however, egg yolk has a supporting role in the thickening thanks to its binding and coagulating properties. Egg yolks also provide emulsification (smoothness), richness, and color.

In many kitchens, the butter is stirred into the pastry cream directly after removing it from the stove. As with many savory sauces, pastry cream is finished with butter for a smooth, creamy mouthfeel and richness. Combining the butter with the pastry cream when they are both just below the melting point of butter will result in a creamier, richer pastry cream.

a Bring the milk and vanilla bean and scrapings to a boil.

d Pour tempered mixture into remaining hot milk.

b Whisk the egg yolks with the cornstarch/sugar mixture.

c Slowly add hot milk to egg yolk paste, stirring constantly.

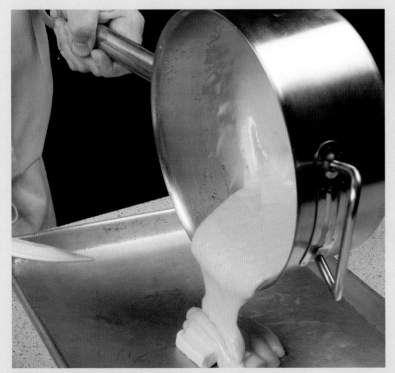

e Pour pastry cream into a shallow container to cool.

f Whisk in the butter.

Yield: One fruit tart

Prep time: active time, 50 minutes; total time, 3 hours

Equipment needed: One or two 9 x 1-inch (23 x 2.5 cm) fluted tart pans, rolling pin, small saucepan, pastry brush

FRUIT TART
BY ROBERT ELLINGER

INGREDIENTS

	U.S. Imperial Weight	Metric Weight	Volume
Engadine nuss torte crust			1 recipe
Chocolate, melted	2 oz	57 g	
Pastry cream	13.9 oz	395 g	
Fruit: fresh berries and assorted firm-fleshed varieties, sliced and diced	1 lb., 1.6 oz	500 g	
Apricot preserves	8 oz	227 g	¾ cup
Simple syrup	6 oz	170 g	¾ cup

PROCEDURE

1 Prepare the engadine nuss torte tart crust as directed on page 76.

2 After the dough has firmed and relaxed in the refrigerator for 2 hours, place it on a lightly floured work surface.

3 Tap the pastry a few times with a rolling pin to soften the dough for rolling.

4 Roll the dough in different directions to create a disc that is approximately 3 inches (7.5 cm) larger than the tart pan. Rotate the dough 90° several times throughout the process and dust the work surface with flour, if necessary.

5 Fold the dough in half and transfer it to the tart pan. Gently press the dough into the fluted sides of the pan (a).

6 Run the rolling pin over the edges to trim the excess dough (b).

7 Place in the refrigerator for 30 minutes to 2 hours to allow the dough to relax, keeping shrinkage at a minimum.

8 Preheat oven to 350°F (180°C or gas mark 4).

9 Remove the dough from the refrigerator and use the tines of a fork to pierce (dock) the dough in the bottom of the pan. Refrigerate for at least 30 minutes.

10 Lay a piece of parchment paper inside the lined tart pan and fill with dry beans or rice.

11 Bake until golden brown, approximately 12 to 15 minutes.

12 Remove the pan from the oven. Remove the parchment liner and beans.

13 Brush the surface of the baked dough with beaten egg and return the pan to the oven for 5 minutes, creating a seal to prolong the crispness of the tart shell after filling with the pastry cream.

a Press the dough into the tart pan.

b Run a rolling pin over the edges to trim.

c Brush a thin layer of melted chocolate over the surface of the dough.

d Fill the shell with an even layer of pastry cream.

(continued)

PROCEDURE (continued)

14 Remove the shell from the oven and place on a cooling rack. When the shell is cool, remove it from the pan and paint the surface of the dough with a thin layer of melted chocolate to ensure a dry, crisp crust (c).

15 Deposit an even layer of pastry cream in the tart shell, filling it 75–80 percent full (d).

16 Arrange fresh fruit in a symmetrical or random pattern on the surface of the pastry cream (e).

17 Combine the apricot preserves and simple syrup in a small saucepan over medium-high heat and boil approximately 1 minute or until the mixture is smooth. Check for doneness: the glaze should flow off a spoon, and when dropped onto a cold plate, it should thicken slightly. Strain and use warm. If the glaze thickens, rewarm and/or thin with more syrup.

18 Using a brush, lightly apply the apricot glaze to the fruit (f). It will seal the fruit, prolonging freshness and maintaining its placement and providing a shiny surface.

19 Refrigerate until service. Fruit tarts are best if eaten the day of preparation.

Rolling the dough out in several directions prevents the dough from sticking and will minimize the possibility of elasticity (shrinkage in the dough)—if the dough is continuously rolled in the same direction, the gluten could develop in one direction, which causes the dough to shrink during baking.

e Arrange the fruit on top of the pastry cream.

f Brush the fruit with apricot glaze.

FLUENT IN FIVE LANGUAGES, JORDI SPENDS MORE TIME TRAVELING THAN HE SPENDS AT HOME. A QUICK STUDY OF HIS CALENDAR INDICATES DATES IN ELEVEN COUNTRIES IN THE COMING MONTHS. AS THE FOUNDER OF SWEET'N GO IN BARCELONA, JORDI SHARES HIS KNOWLEDGE AND EXPERIENCE WITH AN INTERNATIONAL CLIENTELE OF HOTELS, SCHOOLS, BAKERIES, AND PASTRY SHOPS. HE IS AS WELL VERSED IN SAVORY PASTRIES, A GROWING MARKET SEGMENT, AS HE IS IN TRADITIONAL SWEET PASTRY.

JORDI PUIGVERT COLOMER,
FOUNDER OF SWEET'N GO, CONSULTANT, AND PROFESSOR AT THE SCHOOL OF THE HOTEL DE GIRONA IN SPAIN

Jordi has embraced the freethinking characteristic of the modernist movement in cuisine and pastry in Spain. Although his style is fresh and modern, he remains grounded in fundamentals and traditional flavors. Prior to establishing his company, Jordi worked as the pastry chef in two Michelin-starred restaurants and the acclaimed Espai Sucre Restaurant and Dessert School, one of the earliest dessert restaurants. This was one of the proving grounds that blended sweet and savory techniques and flavors.

Since 2006, when he founded Sweet'n Go, Jordi has remained a professor of pastry at the School of the Hotel de Girona, as a demonstrator in the use of pastry ingredients for Comercial Artesana Sosa, and as a pastry consultant for the RIU hotel chain.

Sweet and savoury marriage

INTERVIEW WITH JORDI PUIGVERT COLOMER

HOW DO YOU REMAIN MOTIVATED? HOW DO YOU REMAIN CURRENT?

My job is my passion. When you really like your job, it is very easy to be motivated all the time. I'm remaining current just being motivated, and speaking with pastry chefs around the world with new products and techniques. Also, using new ingredients and techniques, I am able to create something new or just change the methodology of making classic recipes.

OTHER THAN BUTTER, FLOUR, SUGAR, EGGS, AND SALT, WHAT ARE THE FIRST TEN INGREDIENTS YOU WOULD SELECT FOR YOUR KITCHEN?

Chocolate, fruits, spices, milk, cream, starches, yeast, gelatin, almond powder, and praline.

OTHER THAN AN OVEN, WHICH ITEMS ARE ESSENTIAL TO EQUIP YOUR HOME KITCHEN?

Mediterranean flavours

WHAT IS YOUR THOUGHT PROCESS WHEN WRITING A PASTRY MENU?

To build a pastry menu, I try to get different desserts using some ingredients that I think that I cannot miss on the menu. I build desserts using one main ingredient for each one, like chocolate, dairy products, nuts, spices, fruits, and citrus. Once I have all these main ingredients, I create one dessert for each, combining it with other ingredients and using different techniques.

WHAT IS THE FIRST THING YOU TELL A NEW TEAM MEMBER OR STUDENT?

You have to love the work, be passionate, and respect the profession. Otherwise, it makes no sense to go forward. I know that might seem quite aggressive, but students have to know that pastry is not an easy job; they will have to work on Saturdays, Sundays, and almost all holidays.

WHAT ARE THE GUIDING PRINCIPLES/RULES OF YOUR KITCHEN?

Sacrifice, passion, respect, and love.

WHICH GIVES YOU MORE PLEASURE? MAKING PASTRY OR EATING PASTRY?

Both satisfy me. I love the techniques and methodologies. It's exciting to work with the same ingredients and achieve so many different results. I enjoy watching others take pleasure in my creations. At the same time, I love the tastes and aromas of pastries, whether I or someone else made them.

WHAT IS YOUR GREATEST STRENGTH?

My first strength is using the principles and techniques of production when creating my pastries. And the ability to be able to be very polyvalent and flexible when combining sweet and savory techniques in my creations. I studied as a culinary chef as well, and I'm always thinking as a savory chef and as a pastry chef when I'm conceiving my creations.

WORDS TO LIVE BY?

Again, love, passion, respect, and sacrifice.

"You have to love the work, be passionate, and respect the profession. Otherwise, it makes no sense to go forward."

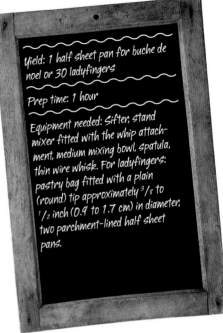

Yield: 1 half sheet pan for buche de noel or 30 ladyfingers

Prep time: 1 hour

Equipment needed: Sifter, stand mixer fitted with the whip attachment, medium mixing bowl, spatula, thin wire whisk. For ladyfingers: pastry bag fitted with a plain (round) tip approximately ³/₈ to ¹/₂ inch (0.9 to 1.7 cm) in diameter; two parchment-lined half sheet pans.

LADYFINGERS/ROULADE
BY JORDI PUIGVERT COLOMER

A simple cake with no fat other than the trace amount found in the egg yolks, this cake is light, tender, and delicate. It can be baked in rounds for layer cakes, as ladyfingers, or in a thin sheet to be used as a roulade.

INGREDIENTS

	U.S. Imperial Weight	Metric Weight	Volume
Cake flour	4.3 oz	122 g	1 cup + 1 teaspoon
Salt	.04 oz	1 g	¹/₈ teaspoon
Egg white			6 egg whites
Granulated sugar	6.5 oz	183 g	1 cup + 2 tablespoons + 1 teaspoon
Egg yolk			6 egg yolks
Vanilla extract			1 tablespoon
Confectioners' sugar, for dusting			

PROCEDURE

1 Preheat oven to 375°F (190°C or gas mark 5). Line two half sheet pans with parchment paper and set aside.

2 Sift the flour and salt three times and reserve.

3 In the bowl of a stand mixer fitted with the whipping attachment, whip the egg whites on medium speed.

4 When the egg whites are frothy, begin adding the sugar gradually.

5 Continue whipping until all the sugar is added and the meringue is shiny and forms a soft peak (a).

6 Reduce the mixing speed to low and incorporate the egg yolks and vanilla extract (b).

7 Remove the bowl from the mixer and fold the flour/salt mixture into the batter (c).

8 For ladyfingers, use a spatula to place the batter in a pastry bag fitted with a medium plain (round) tip (d).

9 Deposit enough batter to fill the bag 60 percent full. Twist the open end of the bag tightly to prevent seepage.

10 With even pressure, pipe approximately 4-inch (10 cm) strips of batter onto the parchment-lined pans (e).

11 Using a sifter or shaker, liberally dust the piped ladyfingers with confectioners' sugar (f).

12 The ladyfingers may be placed in the oven at this point, or you can lift the parchment from the pan and hold it in a vertical position to remove the excess sugar (g). The amount of sugar on the surface of the ladyfingers determines the crust color and contributes to controlling the shape.

13 Bake until the ladyfingers are light golden brown and firm, yet tender.

14 Using a spatula, remove the ladyfingers from the parchment after they have cooled.

15 Store in an airtight container or freeze for future use.

a Whip the egg whites and sugar until the meringue forms a soft peak.

d Fill a pastry bag 60 percent full with the batter.

b Add the egg yolks and vanilla extract.

c Add the flour and fold in with a spatula.

e Pipe the batter in 4-inch (10 cm) strips.

f Generously sprinkle the ladyfingers with confectioners' sugar.

g Lift the parchment paper to shake off excess sugar, if desired.

BÛCHE DE NOËL
BY JORDI PUIGVERT COLOMER

Bûche de Noël is the iconic Christmas cake associated with France. It is universal in its popularity, and the entire family can participate in its simple construction and decoration. Although any flavor combination of cake and filling can be used, this version is classic vanilla and chocolate.

INGREDIENTS

	U.S. Imperial Weight	Metric Weight	Volume
Confectioners' sugar, for dusting	As needed		
Chocolate mousse (see page 89)	1 lb, 8.7 oz–1 lb, 12.2 oz	700 – 800 g	
Chocolate buttercream (see page 96)	1 lb, 6 oz	624 g	⅓ recipe
Cocoa powder, for dusting	As needed		
Italian meringue (see nougat recipe, page 152)			½ recipe

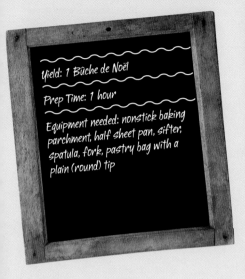

Yield: 1 Bûche de Noël

Prep Time: 1 hour

Equipment needed: nonstick baking parchment, half sheet pan, sifter, spatula, fork, pastry bag with a plain (round) tip

PROCEDURE (see photos, pages 118–120)

1 Preheat oven to 375°F (190°C or gas mark 5).

2 Spread the ladyfingers/roulade batter evenly on a parchment-lined half sheet pan (a, b).

3 Bake until the surface is light golden brown and the edges have pulled away from the pan, approximately 6 to 8 minutes. The cake should spring back when touched in the center and pull away from the sides.

4 Remove from the oven and allow to cool at room temperature.

5 Sift confectioners' sugar onto a sheet of parchment paper.

6 Loosen the cake and remove from the pan (c). Invert it onto the sugar-dusted parchment.

7 Remove the baking parchment from the cake (d).

8 Spread the chocolate mousse (page 89) in an even layer on the exposed surface of the cake (e).

9 Grip and lift the farthest edge of the parchment and use it to begin rolling the filled cake into a cylinder (f).

10 Continue rolling by pulling the parchment upward and toward you, until the bottom edge of the cake is centered on the bottom of the cylinder.

11 Tighten the cylinder by hand (g) or by using a straightedge against the cylinder's edge and pulling the far edge of the parchment away from you (h).

12 Refrigerate the cake until the chocolate mousse is set, approximately 2 to 3 hours.

13 Remove the cake from the refrigerator. Remove the parchment and brush off the excess confectioners' sugar.

14 Slice one end of the cake at an angle (i). Reserve the cut portion to form a stump on the log.

15 Cover the cake with chocolate buttercream (page 96) (j).

16 Place the stump on top of the cake near the uncut end of the log and cover it with the buttercream (k).

17 Drag a fork through the buttercream to create a tree-bark pattern (l).

18 Preheat the oven to 200°F (93°C).

19 Place the meringue in a pastry bag fitted with a medium plain (round) tip. With even pressure, and using the same technique as for piping cream puffs, pipe small bulbs for the caps (m). Use a spoon to smooth out the tops, if necessary (n). With the same pressure, pipe the stems.

20 Lightly dust the mushroom caps with cocoa prior to baking (o).

21 Use a small amount of melted chocolate to attach the stems to the caps.

22 Bake the meringue pieces with the oven door ajar until the meringue is dry, approximately 1 hour.

23 Apply a small amount of buttercream to the bottoms of the mushrooms, and then position them on and around the log.

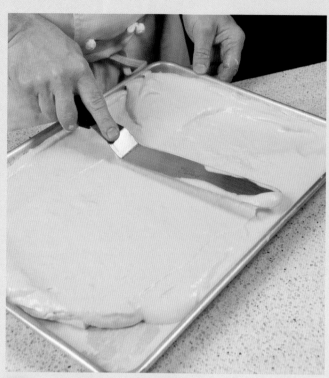

a Pour the batter onto a parchment-lined half sheet pan.

b Spread evenly with an offset spatula.

e Spread chocolate mousse over the cake.

f Use the parchment paper to roll the filled cake into a cylinder.

g Tighten the cylinder by hand.

c Loosen the cake from the pan.

d Remove the parchment from the bottom of the cake.

h Or tighten by holding a straightedge against the cake while pulling on the parchment.

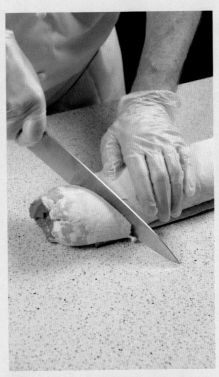

i Cut off one end of the cake at an angle.

j Cover the cake with chocolate buttercream.

(continued)

k Cover the stump with the buttercream.

l Use a fork to create a tree-bark pattern.

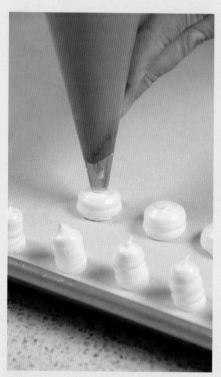

m Pipe meringue for the mushroom caps and stems.

n Smooth out the tops of the caps, if necessary.

o Lightly dust the mushrooms with cocoa.

THOMAS HAAS IS AN ENTERTAINER. WHETHER ENGAGED ONE ON ONE, OR WITH A FULL AUDITORIUM, HE KNOWS HOW TO MAKE PEOPLE HAPPY. HE IS EQUALLY COMFORTABLE ELICITING LAUGHS AND SMILES FROM CHILDREN AS HE IS WITH ADULTS. WITH A ZANY SENSE OF HUMOR, HE TURNS SERIOUS WHEN IT COMES TO PASTRY AND BUSINESS. STARTING WITH NOTHING BUT HIS OWN FUNDING, HE BUILT HIS FIRST SHOP TO COINCIDE WITH THE NEW MILLENNIUM.

THOMAS HAAS,
OWNER OF THOMAS HAAS FINE PASTRIES AND DESSERTS

His began his career at the age of sixteen. After studying and working in his native Germany, Thomas gained experience and developed a global palate by working in Switzerland, France, Canada, and the United States. Along the way, he was the executive pastry chef at the Four Seasons Hotel. Later, Daniel Boloud appointed him as the pastry chef of the Michelin-starred restaurant Daniel in New York City. *Pastry Art & Design* and *Chocolatier* magazines crowned him as one of their top 10 pastry chefs during that time. In 2006, he was honored by Johnson & Wales University as a Distinguished Visiting Chef.

His eponymous shops are known for more than their award-winning chocolates, cakes, and pastries. Wedding cakes, sandwiches, and upscale coffees keep the lines long all day. As a member of the fourth generation of entrepreneurial German bakers, Thomas learned early that service in the shop would satisfy his customers and that service to the community would satisfy his heart.

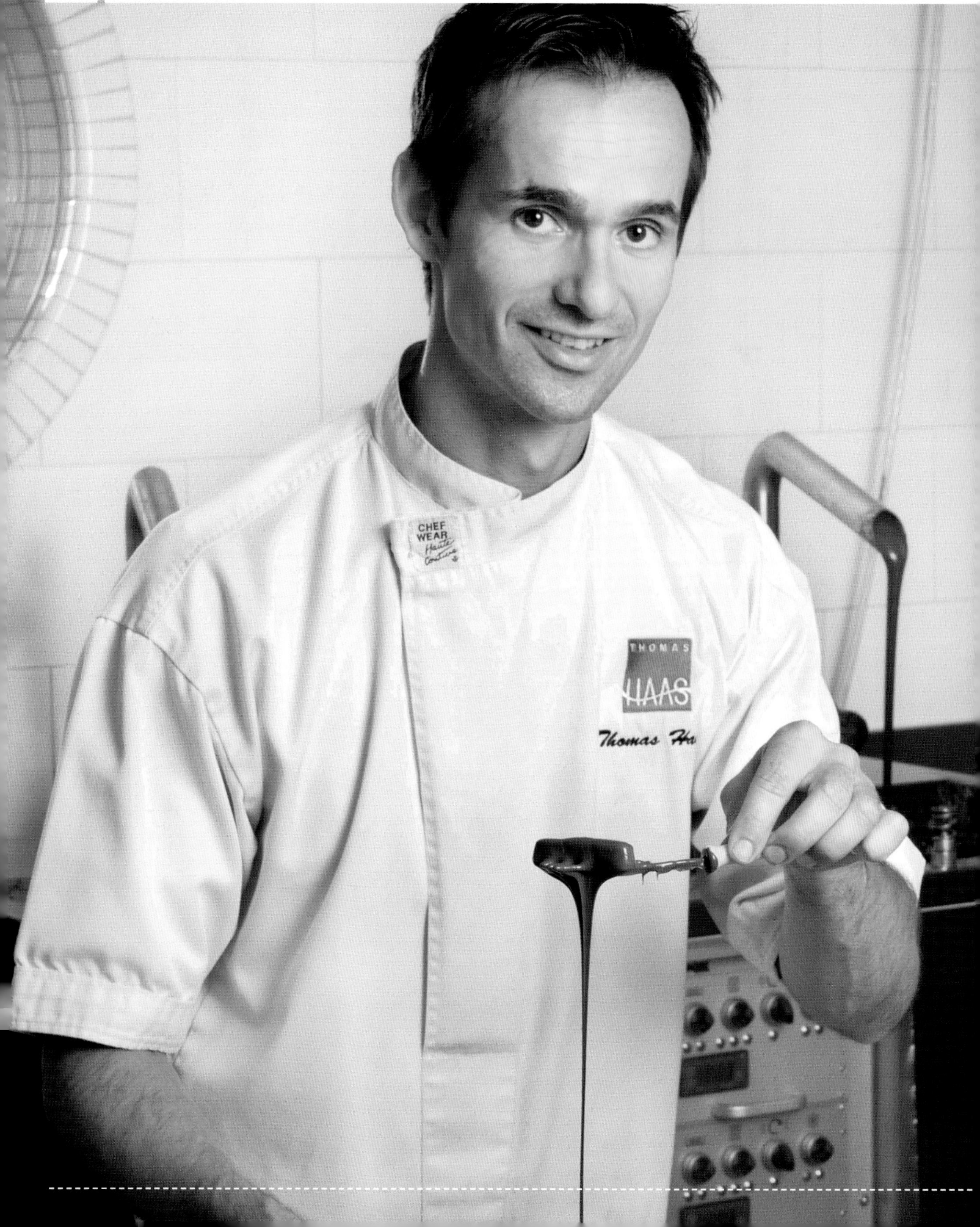
CHEF WEAR Haute Couture
THOMAS HAAS
Thomas Ha

Macarons

INTERVIEW WITH THOMAS HAAS

WHAT WERE YOUR FIRST DUTIES AT YOUR PARENTS' PASTRY SHOP?

Bussing tables, serving drinks, and, on occasion, I would go into the kitchen and do prep for the next day, such as cleaning fruits, lining trays for the baking the next day, and so on.

YOUR INITIAL TRAINING WAS IN GERMANY. HOW DID YOUR EXPERIENCES IN SWITZERLAND, FRANCE, AND NORTH AMERICA COMPARE TO THAT?

In Germany, during my seven years there, I would say that work was dictated by discipline rather than passion. Once your skill level is above-average or near the top, and you take opportunities with responsibilities in highly ranked places, you start fueling your passion and you become aware of the transformation in yourself. It is not possible to differentiate the tastes through the countries I worked in because, in essence, they were all solidly grounded on European techniques and tradition. Of course, the hierarchy is much different in North America. It is more loose, relaxed—and I liked it. I am very sociable and considerate, so I enjoy working like that.

IF SOMEONE WERE TO ASK YOU FOR A RECIPE FOR A TOP-SELLING ITEM IN YOUR SHOP, WOULD YOU SHARE IT?

Of course—we do that all the time. Our best-selling trademarked recipe of a chocolate cookie is all over the Internet for those reasons. What's the point of learning if you don't share?

YOUR STYLE MIRRORS THE COUNTRIES AND CULTURES IN WHICH YOU HAVE LIVED AND WORKED. IS THIS AN ORGANIC OUTGROWTH OF YOUR WORK EXPERIENCE OR A REFLECTION OF THE CULTURE IN WHICH YOU CURRENTLY LIVE?

I think it is a bit of both. You grow and you adapt, but never lose your identity!

SO HOW DO YOU DEFINE YOUR STYLE AND HOW HAS IT EVOLVED OVER THE YEARS?

I think we very much relate to food and ingredients that work well together, flavors and textures that harmonize and please. I do not have pure classical European training. I became a pastry chef way too young at the age of twenty-two and was in charge of a kitchen of fourteen with a team ranging in age from sixteen to fifty-eight. So I really had to wrap my head around a style that was not copied and yet didn't reinvent the wheel. We now run a very successful business with forty staff, and my main thought is "how can we evolve next?" I am hands-on in all aspects of the business, which makes me unable to be at one single place at one time. It would not be wise to get out of my skin when it feels pretty good inside!

HOW DOES YOUR DAY AS AN OWNER/OPERATOR DIFFER FROM BEING THE CORPORATE PASTRY CHEF FOR A LARGE HOTEL OR FOR A RESTAURANT WITH THREE MICHELIN STARS, SUCH AS DANIEL?

Every day is different. I never look back, anyway; that has always benefitted me. Never look back—find the good in the situation you are in and commit to it. This works really well; however, you need to be a bit stubborn.

HOW DO YOU REMAIN MOTIVATED? HOW DO YOU REMAIN CURRENT?

At the beginning, I guess the bank loans keep you motivated, but at the very core, I motivate myself. We have a big responsibility to our clientele and our coworkers. Since we are not trendy, we remain relevant and current much easier!

WHAT ARE THE GUIDING PRINCIPLES/RULES OF YOUR KITCHEN?

Care, care, care, teamwork, care ... and having fun while doing so.

WHAT DO YOU BAKE AT HOME?

Apple tarts in 1,000 different ways with our two kids.

WHAT IS YOUR GREATEST STRENGTH?

People skills and unlimited energy.

WHAT IS YOUR BIGGEST WEAKNESS?

I think I am sometimes too soft and too considerate, which doesn't always get the best out of people, but sometimes it does. And, according to my staff, I am not super-fast in ribboning gift boxes.

WORDS TO LIVE BY?

No dream, no life. Or *Glueck muss man koennen*. ("You can be lucky.")

OTHER THAN BUTTER, FLOUR, SUGAR, EGGS, AND SALT, WHAT ARE THE FIRST TEN INGREDIENTS YOU WOULD SELECT FOR YOUR KITCHEN?

Chocolate, cream, milk, fresh fruits in season, vanilla, almonds, hazelnuts, coffee, mascarpone, and of course, organic quark [a fresh European-style cheese] from the farm.

OTHER THAN AN OVEN, WHICH ITEMS ARE ESSENTIAL TO EQUIP YOUR HOME KITCHEN?

A gas stovetop, a hand blender, a mandolin, a sharp knife set, a fine whisk, and a strainer.

WHAT WAS THE MOST DIFFICULT SKILL FOR YOU TO LEARN WHEN YOU WERE BEGINNING?

Ha! That would be a novel in itself. One day during my apprenticeship I was told to peel a case of apples with a traditional German apple peeler, which is good only for right-handed people (I am left handed). It took me three nights of practice and training to catch up and be faster than my coworkers.

WHAT IS YOUR THOUGHT PROCESS WHEN DEVELOPING A NEW PRODUCT FOR YOUR SHOP?

I imagine what I would like to taste and how it should feel, and then I work backwards.

WHAT IS THE FIRST THING YOU TELL A NEW TEAM MEMBER OR STUDENT?

Learn to love what you do, and learn who you are. Never look back!

"Our best-selling trade-marked recipe of a chocolate cookie is all over the Internet ... What's the point of learning if you don't share?"

Kitsilano, Vancouver, BC, Canada

Yield: Two 9 x 2-inch (23 x 5 cm) cakes, enough for one three-layer torte and one extra layer for future use

Prep time: active time, 20 minutes; total time, 1 hour

Equipment needed: Two 9 x 2-inch (23 x 5 cm) cake pans, stand mixer with paddle attachment, plastic bowl scraper

BLACK FOREST TORTE
UPDATED CLASSIC

Black Forest torte is a staple of German bakeries. It is bold with the flavors of tart cherries, Kirschwasser, and chocolate. It is finished with crème Chantilly, which provides a smooth, slightly sweet, and subtle contrast. This version incorporates sour cream to balance the pH of the recipe—assisting the leavening power of the baking soda, contributing a tangy flavor, extending the keeping qualities, and intensifying the "chocolate" color of the cake.

INGREDIENTS

	U. S. Imperial Weight	Metric Weight	Volume
Unsalted butter*	8.8 oz	248 g	2 sticks + 1 tablespoon
Granulated sugar	9.7 oz	276 g	1¼ cups
Cocoa	3.8 oz	108 g	1 cup
Hot tea			6 tablespoons
Sour cream	8.8 oz	248 g	1 cup
Whole egg			5 large eggs
Vanilla extract			1 tablespoon
Cake flour	6.5 oz	185 g	1¼ cups
Baking soda	0.2 oz	5 g	1 teaspoon
Salt	0.1 oz	4 g	⅝ teaspoon
Chocolate, finely chopped	6.5 oz	185 g	

Recipe note: Use European-style butter (minimum 82% fat content).

PROCEDURE

1 Assemble the ingredients and allow them to come to room temperature.

2 Spray two 9 x 2-inch (23 x 5 cm) cake pans with nonstick cooking spray and line with parchment.

3 Preheat oven to 350°F (180°C or gas mark 4).

4 In the bowl of a stand mixer fitted with the paddle attachment, cream the butter and sugar on medium speed until the mixture is pale yellow, light, and fluffy.

5 Turn the mixer off and add the cocoa. Mix on low speed to combine (a).

6 After the cocoa is incorporated, mix on medium-low speed and add the hot tea gradually, waiting for each addition to be incorporated before adding the next (b). This will prevent cocoa lumps and eliminates the need for the messy sifting of cocoa.

7 Stop the mixer and scrape the bowl and paddle with a bowl scraper.

8 Add the sour cream and incorporate on low speed.

9 Combine the egg and vanilla and add to the batter while mixing on low speed.

10 Stop the mixer and scrape the bowl and paddle.

11 Sift together the cake flour, baking soda, and salt. Add to the batter and mix until just combined.

12 Add the chopped chocolate and mix until just combined (c).

13 Divide the batter between the prepared pans (d), spreading evenly (e).

14 Bake in the center of the oven until a wooden pick inserted in the center of the cakes comes out clean, approximately 22 to 25 minutes.

a The batter will be thick after adding the cocoa.

d Divide the batter between the two prepared pans.

b Add the hot tea slowly.

c Add the finely chopped chocolate.

e Spread the batter evenly.

Any tea may be used to make the cake. Earl Grey goes well with chocolate. Orange, bergamot, and spiced teas also enhance chocolate flavors. Or, you may use plain hot water in place of the tea.

Adding finely chopped chocolate to the cake batter intensifies the chocolate taste without the bitterness, dryness, and toughness often associated with the cocoa. And who doesn't want small flecks of chocolate melting in their mouth?

Yield: 1 pound, 12 ounces (800 g), or enough for one torte with a little left over to garnish the plated slices

Prep time: active time, 20 minutes; total time, 2¹/₂ hours

Equipment needed: 3-quart saucepan, medium mixing bowl, wire whisk

KIRSCH/CHERRY TORTE FILLING

INCLUSIONS

Ingredient	U. S. Imperial Weight	Metric Weight	Volume
Granulated sugar	5.3 oz	150 g	¾ cup + 1 tablespoon + 1 teaspoon
Water	3.5 oz	100 g	¼ cup + 3 tablespoons
Tart cherries in juice	1 lb, 1.6 oz	500 g	1 cup + 1 tablespoon + ¼ teaspoon
Kirschwasser			¼ cup minus 2 teaspoons
Red currant jelly			4 teaspoons
Cornstarch	0.1 oz	3.6 g	

PROCEDURE

1 In a heavy-bottomed pot, combine the sugar, half of the water, the juice of the cherries, and Kirschwasser (a). Cook over medium heat, boiling until the liquid is reduced to a thick syrup (a), approximately 10 to 15 minutes.

2 To check for the proper consistency, place a spoonful of the syrup on a granite surface or a chilled white plate. When the syrup is cool, pull a spoon through it. If the streak from the spoon remains open, the syrup is ready (b).

3 Add the red currant jelly to the pot and melt over medium heat.

4 Make a slurry with the remaining water and cornstarch. Add it to the boiling cherry/ syrup mixture. Cook until thick and clear, approximately 3 to 4 minutes.

5 Add the drained cherries.

6 Cool and reserve (c).

ASSEMBLING THE TORTE

1 Cut each cake in half horizontally, creating four layers. Wrap one layer in plastic and refrigerate or freeze for future use.

2 Place one layer on a cake circle or serving platter. Brush the layer with a mixture of equal parts kirschwasser and simple syrup.

3 Use a pastry bag to pipe concentric circles of crème Chantilly on the cake top. Spoon cherry filling between the circles of crème Chantilly (d).

4 Place a second cake layer on the crème/cherry filling. Brush the cake with the syrup mixture. Repeat step 3, then add a third cake layer. Brush the third layer with the syrup mixture.

5 Using an icing spatula, apply a thin coat of crème Chantilly to the top and sides of the cake, creating a crumb coat. This prevents crumbs on the outside of the cake. Freeze until firm.

6 Remove the cake from the freezer. Using an icing spatula, cover the sides and surface of the cake with an even coat of crème Chantilly.

7 Using a pastry bag fitted with a star tip, pipe rosettes of crème Chantilly around the top edge.

8 Rinse, drain, and dry maraschino cherries. Place the cherries on the rosettes.

9 If desired, use a paper cornet to pipe decorative melted chocolate on the torte.

10 Apply chocolate shavings to the sides of the torte.

11 Freeze until 30 minutes prior to service.

a Add the juice of the cherries and boil until thickened.

b Test the consistency of the syrup.

c Remove cherry mixture from heat and let cool.

d Assembling the torte.

KIM PARK, THE CAPTAIN OF PASTRY TEAM SOUTH KOREA, HAS TIME TO MAINTAIN TWO SUCCESSFUL CAREERS: ONE AS A PASTRY CHEF AND ONE AS A FEATURED PERFORMER IN A SOUTH KOREAN DRAMATIC SERIES. ACCORDING TO HIM, THESE TWO SEEMINGLY DISPARATE DISCIPLINES HAVE MORE IN COMMON THAN A CURSORY GLANCE MIGHT REVEAL. THEY BOTH REQUIRE A LOT OF PRACTICE, DISCIPLINE, AN UNDERSTANDING OF FUNDAMENTALS, AND MOST IMPORTANTLY, THEY PROVIDE PLEASURE.

KIM PARK,
OWNER OF THE GREEN HOUSE BAKERY AND CAPTAIN OF SOUTH KOREA'S NATIONAL PASTRY TEAM

Kim began his baking career working in a shop at the age of fifteen. After thirteen years of working in positions with increasing responsibilities and skill levels, he opened his first bakery, the Green House Bakery. Pressed to make a decision on how the business would survive a time of hardship, he opened a second bakery. Both locations continue to thrive.

To remain current and relevant, Kim began attending national and international competitions to observe new trends and techniques. He found more than recipes and techniques—he found the desire to push himself even farther. He has won six prominent awards in professional competitions and is preparing for the next stage of his competition career: judging. In the meantime, he has two careers to keep him busy.

"A pastry chef is someone who must have the endurance and the courage to dedicate his life to one path. A pastry chef must have a strong work ethic and proper education, have receptive senses, and learn to train his or her sense of taste."

INTERVIEW WITH KIM PARK
Translated by Ok-Kyung Choo, BS, MA

HOW DID YOU DETERMINE YOUR CAREER CHOICE OF BEING A PASTRY CHEF AT THE AGE OF SIXTEEN?

Initially, it was never my intention to become a bakery chef. I was sent to work at a bakery with my parents' approval. When I was a child, we didn't have much, so my parents thought if I worked at a bakery shop, I would never go hungry. They were very supportive and extremely happy that I was able to work at a bakery shop.

PLEASE DESCRIBE YOUR CAREER PATH FROM THE BEGINNING UNTIL YOU OPENED THE GREEN HOUSE BAKERY, YOUR FIRST SHOP.

From the age of sixteen, I worked at a bakery shop gaining hands-on experience, which became my official training. When I turned twenty-eight, I met my wife and got married. That is when I decided to start a personal savings account with the dream of opening my own business. At the age of thirty, we didn't have much money, but we opened a small bakery. For about six months the business was so bad that we worried that we would lose all of our savings. We could not just sit back and watch our business fail, so we saved all that we could and decided to open another location, which is our current Green House Bakery. We worked really hard each and every day to achieve success.

WHAT WERE YOUR THOUGHTS THE NIGHT BEFORE OPENING DAY?

In my mind, I had a vision of where I would be in ten years. I wanted to have the most successful bakery shop in Kim Hae [a small town in Kyung Sang-do, Korea].

WHAT WAS THE FOCUS OF THAT FIRST BAKERY?

The main focus of the shop became the Korean-style shaved ice dessert dish called Pap-Bing Soo. It has shaved ice, ice cream, sweet red beans, strawberries, mango, kiwi, blueberries, raspberries, and other fruits. Pap-Bing Soo and the combination of the pastries led to the success of the Green House Bakery. People started raving about the pure taste and the quality of our pastries.

HOW WOULD YOU DEFINE A PASTRY CHEF?

I would say that a pastry chef is someone who must have the endurance and the courage to dedicate his or her life to one path. A pastry chef must have a strong work ethic and proper education, have receptive senses, and learn to train his or her sense of taste.

HOW IS THE PROFESSIONAL PASTRY CHEF VIEWED BY KOREAN SOCIETY? HAS THIS CHANGED OVER THE YEARS? ARE YOUNG PEOPLE BECOMING MORE INTERESTED IN THE PROFESSION?

Many years ago, being a pastry chef was not something you would rave about as a career. But this has changed over the years and is definitely still changing. With more interest in the pastry industry by the public and the media, we have soap operas such as *Pastry King* that help to facilitate more attention. The younger generation is becoming more interested because of more awareness and the popularity of pastry in Korea.

PLEASE DEFINE YOUR STYLE.

I would have to say that my style is the art-work of my hands. It is unique to me, and I am constantly challenging myself to evolve.

OTHER THAN BUTTER, FLOUR, SUGAR, EGGS, AND SALT, WHAT ARE THE FIRST TEN INGREDIENTS YOU WOULD SELECT FOR YOUR PASTRY KITCHEN?

I love using almonds, hazelnuts, pecans, green tea, red beans, wild cherries, sour cream, pumpkin, sweet potatoes, and potatoes.

OTHER THAN AN OVEN, WHICH ITEMS ARE ESSENTIAL TO EQUIP YOUR HOME KITCHEN?

I would need my mixer, ice cream freezer, candy freezer, and doughnut deep fryer.

WHAT IS YOUR THOUGHT PROCESS WHEN CHOOSING ITEMS TO MAKE FOR YOUR SHOP?

I want to make something that leaves a lasting impression on the customers. Presentation is very important, as is the taste. It must be attractive to the eye for someone to choose the product, and then the taste must follow. Colors can be obtained by using natural fruits and nuts. The shapes must be organic.

WHAT IS THE FIRST THING YOU TELL A NEW TEAM MEMBER OR STUDENT? WHAT ARE THE GUIDING PRINCIPLES/RULES OF YOUR KITCHEN?

Most importantly, make the pastry as if you were to consume it yourself. Pastry is not something that you just produce in the factory, but in fact pastry is a very intricate cooking process. Think only of pastry and nothing else. Stay focused.

WORDS TO LIVE BY?

Love what you do, do what you love, and make sure to make time for those you love.

MADELEINES
BY KIM PARK

What if Proust had never tasted or written about madeleines? Would they be as popular as they are now? Actually, madeleines were a favorite treat in high society Versailles in the early 1700s. They may be baked lightly for a tender cake or baked to a darker color for a drier, more flavorful cake with a slightly crisp crust to be dipped in coffee or tea.

INGREDIENTS

	U.S. Imperial Weight	Metric Weight	Volume
Unsalted butter, for molds*	As needed		
Unsalted butter	6 oz	170 g	1½ sticks
Bread flour	4 oz	113 g	½ cup
Pastry flour	4 oz	113 g	½ cup
Baking powder	0.2 oz	5 g	1 tablespoon
Salt	0.2 oz	5 g	¾ teaspoon
Whole egg**			5 eggs
Granulated sugar	6 oz	170 g	¾ cup
Vanilla bean			1 bean

Recipe notes: *Use European-style butter (minimum 82% fat content).
**Eggs should be at room temperature.

PROCEDURE

1 Melt a small amount of butter and leave in a cool place to thicken.

2 Brush madeleine molds with thickened butter (a). Set aside.

3 Preheat oven to 400°F (200°C or gas mark 6).

4 Melt the 6 ounces (170 g) of butter and reserve.

5 Sift together the flours, baking powder, and salt. Reserve.

6 In the bowl of a stand mixer fitted with the whip attachment, whip the eggs and sugar until they are pale yellow, thick, and form a ribbon when you lift the whip (b).

7 Scrape the vanilla bean and add scrapings to the mixture.

8 Remove the whip attachment and replace it with the paddle attachment. (This prevents incorporating excess air, which would affect the texture of the baked madeleines.)

9 Continue to mix on low speed, adding the sifted flour mixture gradually (c).

10 Remove one-third of the mixture from the bowl and stir the melted 6 ounces (170 g) of butter into it (d).

11 Add the butter/batter mixture to the batter remaining in the bowl and mix lightly (e).

12 Use a spatula to place the mixture in a pastry bag fitted with a medium plain (round) tip.

13 Using medium pressure, pipe the mixture into the prepared molds (f).

14 For symmetrical madeleines without the traditional hump, bake directly. For madeleines with a hump, refrigerate the filled pans for 1½ hours prior to baking. Alternatively, the batter may be refrigerated for 1½ hours and then piped into the molds.

15 When ready to bake, preheat oven to 400°F (200°C or gas mark 6) oven and bake until golden brown, approximately 13 to 15 minutes.

16 While they are still warm, tap the molds on a solid surface to remove the madeleines (g).

17 When the madeleines are cool, dust with confectioners' sugar (h).

If you have only one madeleine pan, reserve the unused batter in an airtight container in the refrigerator. After the first round of madeleines has been baked, cool the pan, wash or wipe it clean, brush with butter, fill, and bake again. Double acting baking powder will remain dormant until the madeleine batter is placed in the oven; it will activate when it is exposed to the heat of the oven.

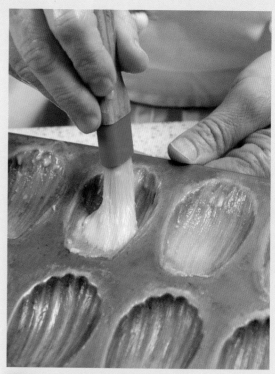

a Brush the madeleine molds with butter.

e Combine the butter mixture with the remaining batter.

b The batter should form a ribbon when you lift the whip.

c Add the sifted flour mixture to the batter.

d Stir the melted butter into one-third of the batter.

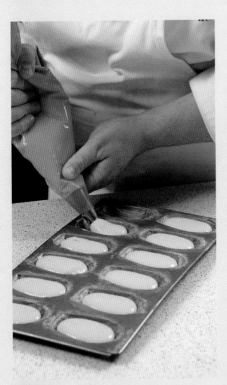

f Pipe the batter in 4-inch (10 cm) strips.

g Tap the molds on a solid surface to release the madeleines while they are still warm.

h Sprinkle the cooled madeleines with confectioners' sugar.

ANIL ATTENDED BOMBAY UNIVERSITY AND THE INSTITUTE OF HOTEL MANAGEMENT AND CATERING TECHNOLOGY IN INDIA BEFORE SPENDING TWO YEARS WITH AN AIRLINE CATERER. TO BUILD ON HIS CULINARY KNOWLEDGE, HE ENROLLED AT THE CULINARY INSTITUTE OF AMERICA TO STUDY BAKING AND PASTRY. HE GRADUATED IN 1995 AND WORKED FOR SEVERAL HIGH-PROFILE ORGANIZATIONS BEFORE ACCEPTING A POSITION AS A TEACHING ASSISTANT TO EWALD NOTTER.

ANIL ROHIRA,
CORPORATE PASTRY CHEF FOR FELCHLIN AND COACH AND JUDGE FOR NATIONAL AND INTERNATIONAL COMPETITIONS

Longing for the sense of urgency only a pastry kitchen can provide, Anil accepted an offer to become the executive pastry chef at the Chevy Chase Country Club in Washington DC. One year later, he became the corporate pastry chef for Albert Uster Imports. Most recently, he accepted a position to represent Felchlin, the Swiss-based chocolate manufacturer. He provides consultation, education, support, and advice to its clientele.

Anil is appreciated for his warmth and generosity. At the World Pastry Forum, he stops for everyone—stranger, colleagues, and peers—sharing his knowledge and expertise. He maintains a standard of excellence in the kitchen that few can achieve. In competitions, he is calm, focused, and smiling, finding the time to greet observers, judges, and media.

Between 1997 and 1999, he won four gold medals in American Culinary Federation competitions. In 2000, he competed at the National Pastry Team Championship in Beaver Creek, Colorado, where he won the bronze medal. In 2003, he was the team captain of the U.S. team at the *Coupe du Monde de la Patisserie*. He received the judges' prize for the best sugar showpiece. In 2009, he was recognized as the pastry chef of the year while judging at the National Pastry Team Championship. He continues to coach and judge at national and international championships.

"I think competitions support innovation and development. A lot of new techniques, flavors, textures, and presentations are seen at these events."

INTERVIEW WITH ANIL ROHIRA

YOU ARE REGARDED AS AN EXPERT ON CHOCOLATES, CHOCOLATE SHOWPIECES, AND SUGAR SHOWPIECES. HOW WERE YOU ABLE TO MASTER SO MUCH?

I am far from being a master at our craft. Whether it is designing a showpiece, composing desserts, working on confections, or laminating dough, it is all very exciting for me. I have been fortunate to work with acclaimed chefs at highly reputed places. I have had the opportunities to develop my skills in all areas of the craft. There is not an area in baking and pastry that I can say does not motivate me. No matter how long one is in a business, there is always lots to learn, which is the fascinating part of our profession.

WHAT DOES BEING A PASTRY CHEF MEAN?

You can look at this question from many different perspectives. Being a pastry chef is a career path you make because you are motivated and dedicated to do well in the field of baking and pastry. Your responsibility to yourself is to do your best to further your skills and knowledge and to serve and/or present your guests with the best possible desserts. You should be a good educator to your team and staff, and you have a responsibility to your company to do your best to be profitable.

HOW DOES THE PUBLIC IN INDIA PERCEIVE THE PROFESSION OF BEING A PASTRY CHEF?

The world is a much smaller place today. People are well traveled and aware of international cuisine. India, in particular, is a booming economy. There is a lot of awareness of good food, healthy eating, and quality products. There are a number of international hotels that have opened in India and are rapidly expanding. With all this growth, the perception of a pastry chef has changed as well. It is not like it was ten to fifteen years ago. The chefs are out in front, and there are more channels showcasing food and chefs. Today, there are tremendous opportunities for pastry chefs and bakers in India.

WHAT TYPES OF DESSERTS ARE COMMON IN INDIAN HOMES?

Desserts in India are going through a period of transition. Traditionally, desserts in India were rich. Fats, sugars, and nuts played a big role in their makeup. We did not always have the best conditions to store desserts, so sugar and fats were used as preservatives. Today things are different. Desserts have a Western flair to them. There are different opportunities and options. Chocolate and pastry shops are very accessible.

WHAT IS THE MOST SATISFYING PART OF YOUR JOB?

The most satisfying part about my job is that I have the opportunity to be a part of this industry on a global level. I work with chefs in different parts of the world and get to understand different cultures and try to find ways of servicing their needs and tastes. Creating desserts becomes very exciting in different parts of the world. Working with changing ingredients, especially local fruits and flavors, is exciting. There is always something to learn.

HOW DO YOU REMAIN MOTIVATED? HOW DO YOU REMAIN CURRENT?

There is just so much to learn and enjoy, how can one not be motivated?

OTHER THAN BUTTER, FLOUR, SUGAR, EGGS, AND SALT, WHAT ARE THE FIRST TEN INGREDIENTS YOU WOULD SELECT FOR YOUR KITCHEN?

I'll list five: chocolate, fruits, nuts, vanilla, and good music.

OTHER THAN AN OVEN, WHICH ITEMS ARE ESSENTIAL TO EQUIP YOUR HOME KITCHEN?

A digital scale, a whisk, a heat-resistant spatula, a thermometer, a stand mixer, a set of nice bowls, and we are ready to bake.

WHAT ARE THE GUIDING PRINCIPLES/RULES OF YOUR KITCHEN?

Teamwork. Hard work. Good desserts.

WHAT IS YOUR GREATEST STRENGTH? WHAT IS YOUR BIGGEST WEAKNESS?

Strength: punctuality. Weakness: no tolerance for lack of effort.

IT'S YOUR CHILD'S BIRTHDAY; WHAT PASTRY OR CAKE DO YOU MAKE?

This is really difficult. I have learned that I have to keep my opinion out and listen to the kids, and to deliver what they ask for. I love to do the décor for their cakes. I get them involved as well. It is a beautiful experience to see them cut the cakes with their friends.

WORDS TO LIVE BY?

Heart, hands, and head. This is what our profession is all about.

Yield: Approximately thirty-six 2 X 2-inch (5 X 5 cm) marshmallows

Prep time: active time 30 to 40 minutes; total time, 13 hours

Equipment needed: 4-quart saucepan, stand mixer with whip attachment, two silicone baking mats, half sheet pan, rolling pin, large chef's knife

MARSHMALLOWS
BY ANIL ROHIRA

Until you've had a marshmallow made the old-fashioned way, you might not fully understand the cult of marshmallow lovers. An artisan-made marshmallow is smooth, light, flavorful, a bit chewy, and creamy. They are a study in subtlety and nuance. Nothing overwhelms, nothing is over the top. And yet, they render the eater speechless.

INGREDIENTS

	U.S. Imperial Weight	Metric Weight	Volume
Sheet gelatin			1⅓ sheets
Ice water, strained			1 cup minus 1 tablespoon
Vanilla bean			2 beans
Water			1 cup minus 1 tablespoon
Glucose	9.9 oz	281 g	¾ cup
Granulated sugar	1 lb, 9 oz	708 g	3¼ cups
Salt	0.05 oz	1.5 g	¼ teaspoon
Cornstarch	6 oz	170 g	⅛ cup
Confectioners' sugar	6 oz	170 g	1⅛ cup

PROCEDURE

1 Line a half-sheet pan with a silicone baking mat. Spray the mat with nonstick cooking spray. Set aside.

2 Place the gelatin in the bowl of a stand mixer and cover with the strained ice water. Soak for ten minutes.

3 Add the scrapings of the vanilla beans.

4 Using the whip attachment, whip the gelatin/water/vanilla mixture on low speed.

5 In a heavy-bottomed pot, cook the water, glucose, and sugar to 238°F (214°C) (a). Then add the salt.

6 Slowly pour the syrup into the gelatin mixture, being careful to avoid the whip and the sides of the bowl (b).

7 After all the syrup has been added, increase the mixing speed to medium-high.

8 Continue whipping until the mixture is cool, thick, and spreadable, approximately 12 to 15 minutes (c).

9 Remove the mixture from the bowl and spread it evenly in the prepared pan (d, e).

10 Spray a second silicone baking mat with nonstick cooking spray. Place the sprayed side on the surface of the marshmallow and use a nontapered rolling pin to roll the mass flat and even (f). Remove the second baking mat.

11 Set the pan aside and reserve at room temperature until firm, at least 3 to 4 hours. For optimum results, leave the pan overnight.

12 Sift together the cornstarch and confectioners' sugar. Sift some of the mixture onto a flat cutting surface (g).

13 Remove the marshmallow from the pan and place it on the sifted starch/sugar mixture. Sift more of the starch/sugar mixture on top of the marshmallow slab (h).

14 Spray the blade of a large chef's knife with nonstick cooking spray. Continue wiping and spraying the knife as needed during the cutting process.

15 Trim the edges of the marshmallow and cut into even squares (i, j).

16 Toss the cut marshmallows in the remaining starch/sugar mixture (k).

a Check the temperature of the glucose mixture with a thermometer.

d Pour the marshmallow mixture onto the prepared baking pan.

b Slowly pour the syrup into the whipped gelatin mixture.

c Note the consistency of the finished marshmallow mixture.

e Spread the marshmallow evenly using an offset spatula.

f Using a rolling pin and a silicone baking mat, roll over the marshmallow until it is flat and even.

(continued)

g Sift confectioners' sugar and cornstarch onto your work surface.

h Sift more of the confectioners' sugar mixture on top of the marshmallow.

i Slice the marshmallow into long strips.

j Slice again, crosswise into squares.

k Toss the marshmallow squares with remaining starch/sugar mixture.

When you pour the sugar syrup into the mixing bowl, avoid getting the syrup on the sides of the bowl or the whip. If it comes in contact with those surfaces, it will remain there—not making it into the gelatin mixture. The amount of syrup in the gelatin mixture will determine the sweetness and texture of the marshmallows.

These marshmallows freeze well. Wrap in a double layer of aluminum foil prior to freezing. Ideally, leave the slab whole and cut as needed, returning the remainder of the slab to the freezer for future use. Thaw the marshmallows to room temperature, then toss in the starch/sugar mixture.

ONE OF THE MOST DECORATED CHEFS IN THE MODERN COMPETITION ERA, EWALD NOTTER IS DIRECTLY AND/OR INDIRECTLY RESPONSIBLE FOR THE LOOK OF CONTEMPORARY PASTRY SCULPTURES AROUND THE WORLD. HIS STYLE HAS BEEN THE MOST WIDELY COPIED AND EMULATED ART FORM IN PASTRY FOR OVER TWO DECADES. ELEVATING HIS SKILLS AND ACHIEVING EXCELLENCE MOTIVATE HIM MORE THAN THE RECOGNITION HE RECEIVES FOR HIS WORK.

EWALD NOTTER,
FOUNDER AND DIRECTOR OF EDUCATION OF NOTTER SCHOOL OF PASTRY ARTS

With so many competitors, hotels, and pastry chefs seeking his advice and expertise, it was only natural that Ewald would found a school, opening first in Switzerland and later in Gaithersberg, Maryland, finally relocating to Orlando. His list of teaching affiliations numbers over thirty schools and associations across five continents. Generous and gentlemanly, he is sought out by those seeking to be the best.

For all of his artistic success, Ewald has not forsaken chocolates and pastries. His first two books were focused on sugar work, the creation of elaborate showpieces using different techniques; however, his most recent book, *The Art of the Chocolatier*, focuses on chocolate confections and showpieces.

INTERVIEW WITH EWALD NOTTER

THE PUBLIC REVERES YOUR SUGAR AND CHOCOLATE SHOWPIECES TO SUCH A DEGREE THAT THEY OVERLOOK THE FACT THAT YOU ARE AN ACCOMPLISHED PASTRY CHEF AND CHOCOLATIER. WHAT WOULD YOU SAY TO THEM?

I had the opportunity to spend more time doing decorations than most other pastry chefs, so it came naturally to be more recognized for my sugar and chocolate creations. I respect and appreciate everyone who follows my passions.

HOW HAS BEING THE DIRECTOR OF A SCHOOL ALTERED YOUR PERCEPTION OF TRAINING, TEACHING, AND EDUCATING?

My perception has not changed. Even as a director, I'm able to work one on one with each student, and the skills and training imparted to each individual are tools that can be used throughout his or her career.

DID YOU HAVE A MENTOR AS YOU WERE COMING UP? ARE YOU STILL IN CONTACT?

Yes. My mentor was Willy Pfund. He was an older gentleman who shared his professional experiences with me and helped develop my hand skills. I appreciated this very much because at that time it was very unusual for most chefs to share their knowledge so deeply. Unfortunately, he passed away some time ago.

HOW HAS YOUR STYLE EVOLVED OVER TIME?

My style used to be very traditional European classic, but now the styles have changed from competing and working with different guest chefs. The styles have become trendy and contemporary. This is what we like to teach in the classes: starting with traditional baking [and progressing] to modern and trendy techniques.

OTHER THAN BUTTER, FLOUR, SUGAR, EGGS, AND SALT, WHAT ARE THE FIRST TEN INGREDIENTS YOU WOULD SELECT FOR YOUR KITCHEN?

Fruit, chocolate, heavy cream, vanilla, spirits, cocoa butter, cornstarch, glucose, gelatin, and yeast.

OTHER THAN AN OVEN, WHICH ITEMS ARE ESSENTIAL TO EQUIP YOUR KITCHEN?

A hand blender, a stand mixer, a metric scale, a torch, an infrared thermometer, and piping bags.

WHAT WAS THE MOST DIFFICULT SKILL FOR YOU TO LEARN WHEN YOU WERE BEGINNING?

Patience with myself.

WHAT IS YOUR THOUGHT PROCESS WHEN WRITING A PASTRY MENU?

I have to consider the season of the year, the venue, the type of function, and the number of guests.

WHAT ARE THE GUIDING PRINCIPLES/RULES OF YOUR KITCHEN?

Clean as you go.

WHAT IS YOUR GREATEST STRENGTH? WHAT IS YOUR BIGGEST WEAKNESS?

Strength: decisiveness. Weakness: patience.

WORDS TO LIVE BY?

You are only as good as you are today.

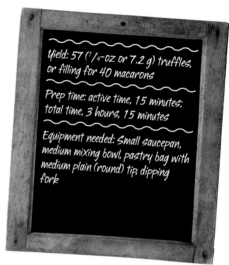

Yield: 57 ($^1/_4$-oz or 7.2 g) truffles, or filling for 40 macarons

Prep time: active time, 15 minutes; total time, 3 hours, 15 minutes

Equipment needed: Small saucepan, medium mixing bowl, pastry bag with medium plain (round) tip, dipping fork

MILK CHOCOLATE TRUFFLES
BY EWALD NOTTER

INGREDIENTS

	U.S. Imperial Weight	Metric Weight	Volume
Milk chocolate couverature	1 lb, 4 oz	567 g	
Heavy cream			1 cup
Glucose	1 oz	28 g	⅛ cup
Confectioners' sugar, for dusting			
Milk chocolate couverature, for dipping			

Truffles are named for their resemblance to the mushroomlike delicacy. With care and respect, they are easy to produce in their simplest form: a ganache made from cream and chocolate and a coating of tempered chocolate. Without other flavorings, such as liqueurs, nuts, spices, etc., there is nothing to interfere with the pure flavor of chocolate. Most chocolate manufacturers are producing high-quality milk chocolate in which the chocolate is not masked or overwhelmed by the addition of milk and sugar. The label will indicate the percentage of cocoa butter and cacao solids. Look for a percentage ranging from 33 to 38 percent or higher.

PROCEDURE

1 Chop the 1 lb, 4 oz (567 g) of couveralture and place in a bowl.

2 Place the cream and glucose in a heavy-bottomed pot and heat just to a boil.

3 Pour the cream/glucose mixture over the chopped couverature (a).

4 Stir smooth with a spatula (b).

5 Cover and cool to room temperature.

6 When the ganache is cool and set, use a rubber spatula to stir the mixture until it lightens in texture and color (c).

7 Place the mixture in a pastry bag fitted with a medium plain (round) tip (d) and pipe ¾-inch (1.9 cm) rounds on a parchment-lined sheet pan (e).

8 Refrigerate until firm. When the ganache is firm, remove the pan from the refrigerator.

9 Wearing latex or vinyl gloves dusted with confectioners' sugar, hand-roll the piped ganache into small spheres (f).

10 Return the spheres to the pan and return the pan to the refrigerator.

a Pour the hot cream/glucose mixture over the chopped chocolate.

d Place ganache in a pastry bag.

b Stir smooth with a spatula.

c Stir the ganache until it lightens in texture and color.

e Pipe rounds of ganache onto a parchment-lined sheet pan.

f Hand-roll the ganache into spheres.

(continued)

PROCEDURE (continued)

11 Temper more couverature (see page 27 for instructions on tempering chocolate).

12 Remove the truffles from the refrigerator.

13 Using gloved hands, spread a small amount of tempered couverature on your palms.

14 Roll the spheres gently to coat evenly (g).

15 Return the truffles to the sheet pan and leave at room temperature to let the couverature set.

16 Using a dipping fork, dip the truffles in the remaining tempered milk couverature.

17 Return the truffles to the sheet pan and allow the couverature to set (h).

18 If desired, the truffles may be rolled across a wire screen after dipping for a spiked appearance. While the couverature is soft, place the truffles on a cooling screen or grid. Use the tip of dipping fork or a paring knife to roll the truffle across the grid to form the spikes.

Ganache is an emulsion of cream and chocolate or couverature. It is often used as a filling, such as in these truffles, or in cakes, tortes, and pastries. It can be used as an icing or a poured glaze for cakes and pastries as well. Incorporating glucose slows or prevents moisture loss and allows the ganache to keep its shine when used as a glaze.

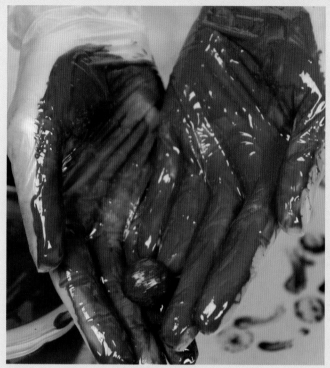

g Coat the spheres with tempered couverature.

h Truffles after the couverature has set.

MENTION THE NAME LAUREN HAAS TO HER FRIENDS AND COLLEAGUES, AND THE SUPERLATIVES FLOW. THE MIDDLE OF THREE SISTERS, SHE BEGAN BAKING AT HOME WHEN SHE WAS TEN YEARS OLD. FIRST, IT WAS DESSERT FOR THE FAMILY MEAL, TREATS FOR SNACKING, AND THE OCCASIONAL BREAKFAST PASTRY. AS HER FASCINATION GREW, SHE BEGAN MAKING SOPHISTICATED PASTRIES AND CAKES FOR FRIENDS TO CELEBRATE BIRTHDAYS OF FRIENDS AND FAMILY. SLOWLY, SHE REALIZED SHE WAS DESTINED FOR A CAREER IN PASTRY.

LAUREN V. HAAS,
ASSISTANT PASTRY CHEF AT ALBERT USTER IMPORTS AND INSTRUCTOR AT JOHNSON & WALES UNIVERSITY

"Relationships are the nucleus of the baking and pastry trade. The advice I would give to those starting in the profession is to gain as much exposure in the industry as possible and to cultivate relationships."

When she reached high school, the decision was made to homeschool her with her younger sister. Her dream was to graduate and then attend culinary school. Wisely, she decided to test the waters before committing and found a job in a local bakery. She knew nothing about the owner, who happened to be an accomplished pastry chef with experience in four-star hotels and pastry shops.

Her first position was in the front of the house, greeting customers and filling orders. Eventually, she began preparing buttercream and scooping cookies. When the owner heard of her plans, he persuaded her to remain at the bakery, offering to train her.

When it was time to enroll in school, Lauren's mother was ill. She decided to remain at home to be close to her family. After three years of intensive training at the bakery, she realized that she had the skills to succeed.

HOW WERE YOU ABLE TO OBTAIN EXPERIENCE IN WORLD-CLASS KITCHENS AT SUCH A YOUNG AGE?

In the early stages of my career, I was hungry to learn and often worked two or more jobs at a time. I went to every food- and pastry-related event that I could find and introduced myself to people in the industry. You meet someone who knows someone else, and suddenly you have a job opportunity. A lot of it is being in the right place at the right time. Relationships are the nucleus of the baking and pastry trade. Relationships with one's clientele, vendors, and other professionals are essential. The advice I would give to those starting in the profession is to gain as much exposure in the industry as possible and to cultivate relationships.

HOW WOULD YOU DEFINE A PASTRY CHEF?

A pastry chef is one who derives great pleasure from serving others. Pastry chefs are in the business of making people happy with their sweet creations. Our creations are ephemeral. They cannot be displayed for posterity.

WHAT IS YOUR PASTRY-MAKING STYLE?

I like to take modern techniques and apply them to classic pastries. Classics are classics because the flavor and texture combinations work well. For example, black forest cake [contains] chocolate, cherries, vanilla whipped cream, and kirsch. It's a great combination, but presenting those flavors as a wedge of cake can be a cliché. You could make a cherry-kirsch sorbet and serve it with a chocolate crumble and a vanilla mousse.

SHOULD ONE LEARN TO MAKE THE CAKE FIRST?

Absolutely. If you don't understand the fundamentals, you won't be able to understand how and why things work. That understanding provides you with the ability to create.

INTERVIEW WITH LAUREN V. HAAS

DO YOU FEEL THAT HAVING BEEN HOMESCHOOLED GIVES YOU SPECIFIC TRAITS THAT CARRY OVER TO THE JOB OF PASTRY CHEF?

Homeschooling requires self-motivation, which has clearly carried over into my job as a pastry chef. As a homeschooler, I did not have other students to compare myself to or teachers to push me. I realize that was valuable training to continue pushing my personal limits.

DO YOU THINK THAT THE ABSENCE OF A TRADITIONAL FORMAL EDUCATION HELPS OR HINDERS YOU IN TRAINING AND/OR TEACHING?

A generation before me, many pastry chefs may have said that they preferred to hire someone who did *not* go to culinary school [because they had] fewer bad habits. The first chef I worked with was of this school of thought, and I ended up staying and working at his pastry shop for three years. It was there that I learned many of the basic skills that have allowed me to go so far. In the past ten or twenty years, things have changed dramatically in our industry and in the job market, and having a culinary degree has become almost essential.

HOW DO YOU REMAIN MOTIVATED? HOW DO YOU REMAIN CURRENT?

It is not possible to travel everywhere to see what is new in the industry, so reading is a great way to stay current. Magazines, newspapers, the Internet, and books are full of ideas, trends, and inspiration.

OTHER THAN BUTTER, FLOUR, SUGAR, EGGS, AND SALT, WHAT ARE THE FIRST TEN INGREDIENTS YOU WOULD SELECT FOR YOUR KITCHEN?

Vanilla beans—there is nothing that can replace the taste and smell of real vanilla beans; it's simply intoxicating. High-quality chocolate—you cannot make fine chocolate candies or decorations using chocolate chips. A variety of fresh fruits—having fresh fruit on hand is the easiest way to be inspired. It is easy to make something that tastes good when you have fresh, juicy fruits. Demerara, muscovado, and other sugars impart different textures and flavor profiles. They provide a unique look and a nice crunch to streusels and toppings. Yogurt is healthy and gives a tang to both sweet and savory foods. Walnut and hazelnut oil are a great way to add depth and flavor to anything from cakes to frying. Liquors add a nice punch and dress up any dessert. Cinnamon sticks, whole nutmeg, whole cloves, and cardamom seeds in their pods—having these spices unground makes them ideal for infusions. Ground spices can have a "dusty" flavor. It is better to grate your own nutmeg, crack the cardamom pod, etc. A variety of flours (whole wheat, pastry, cake, and bread) gives you the ability to have control over the final baked product, whether you choose to add flavor with whole wheat or keep your cake white and tender with cake flour. Almond flour adds fat, texture, and flavor to baked goods.

OTHER THAN AN OVEN, WHICH ITEMS ARE ESSENTIAL TO EQUIP YOUR KITCHEN?

Two or three silicone spatulas, which are flexible enough to scrape every last bit of whipped cream from a bowl but can also withstand high heat. They are fantastic for cooking and sautéing and more sanitary than the traditional wooden spoon.

Professional-grade half sheet pans—many home baking pans are too thin, causing cookies and other items to burn on the bottom before cooking through. A professional-grade sheet pan is much thicker, so it protects the bottom of baked goods and conducts heat more evenly. They last forever and withstand a lot of abuse.

A spiral whisk has an offset handle and a spiral coil. Unlike a traditional whisk, it efficiently reaches to all the corners of a pot and quickly breaks up yolks or whips cream.

An immersion blender is great for making everything from a vinaigrette to a smoothie. I use the attachments for grinding coffee, spices, and nuts.

Bins/canisters for dry ingredients keep everything looking organized, prevent contamination, and make scooping and measuring easier.

Stainless steel bowls in four or five different sizes that nest into each other. You will have them for the rest of your life. I have my grandmother's set.

Finally, a knife you love. Some knives just feel great in your hand. It is a combination of its weight and the shape and material of the handle. Find one you love and take care of it. It will last your lifetime.

WHAT IS THE FIRST THING YOU TELL A NEW TEAM MEMBER OR STUDENT?

Work clean and have your *mise en place* in order before starting a project! Your colleagues will appreciate and respect you if you work clean and are organized.

WHAT ARE THE GUIDING PRINCIPLES/RULES OF YOUR KITCHEN?

Teamwork.

WHAT DO YOU BAKE AT HOME?

If I am baking at home, it will always be comfort foods—jams from scratch, a rustic fruit pie, or cookies.

WHAT WOULD YOUR FANTASY PASTRY VACATION BE?

I would travel to a cacao plantation to learn firsthand how cocoa beans are grown, harvested, and processed. Most chocolate is made up of 50 to 80 percent pure cocoa bean. Cocoa is an important global commodity, and millions of people around the world depend on it for their livelihood. The trend is to get to the source of our foods. I appreciate the cultural and historical aspects of ingredients, especially cocoa.

WHICH GIVES YOU MORE PLEASURE? MAKING PASTRY OR EATING PASTRY?

It is hard to separate the two, as they are connected. I would say eating pastry. The more effort and skill that goes into making something, the more pleasure I have in eating it. One of my favorite things to eat is a good croissant. Though croissants can be found in almost any bakeshop, it takes an incredible amount of skill and attention to make one that is truly good. When I find one, eating it is one of the greatest pleasures.

HOW DO YOU STAY MOTIVATED?

It can be tempting to feel comfortable and complacent. I find that if I am around people I admire professionally, it pushes me to improve my skills and reach for the next level. These people are not always in my backyard, so I like to travel, see new things, and meet other pastry chefs.

WORDS TO LIVE BY?

Whatever you decide to do, do it with your whole heart. The closer you get to your potential, the greater your potential becomes.

Yield: 3 pounds, 1.9 ounces (1,415 g).
Makes 49 (1-ounce or 28 g)
squares or 24 (2-ounce or 57 g)
rectangles.

Prep time: active time, 25 to 30
minutes; total time, 2½ hours

Equipment needed: Stand mixer with
whip attachment, 2 heavy-bottomed
pots, medium-size bowl, large chef's
knife

NOUGAT
BY LAUREN V. HAAS

Variations of nougat are made in European communities as a means to celebrate and preserve the flavors of spring and summer. This recipe uses Italian meringue to provide structure, consistency, and shelf life to a chewy, creamy celebration of local ingredients

INCLUSIONS

	U.S. Imperial Weight	Metric Weight	Volume
Dried blueberries	4.6 oz	130 g	1 cup
Pistachios	6 oz	170 g	1¼ cups
Candied violet petals	3 oz	85 g	¾ cup
Freeze-dried strawberries, chopped	1.7 oz	50 g	½ cup
Salt	Pinch	Pinch	Pinch

INGREDIENTS

	U.S. Imperial Weight	Metric Weight	Volume
Dried egg white	0.4 oz	10 g	1 tablespoon
Granulated sugar	14.4 oz	410 g	1⅞ cups
Fresh egg white			1⅓ egg whites
Honey			1 cup
Glucose syrup			½ cup
Water			6 tablespoons + 2 teaspoons
Vanilla bean	1 bean	1 bean	1 bean
Cocoa butter, melted	1.8 oz	50 g	
Rose water			2 teaspoons
Confectioners' sugar, for dusting			
Tempered couverture for dipping (optional, page 27)			

PROCEDURE

1 Prepare the inclusions: Gently stir together the inclusions in a heatproof bowl and place in a warm oven (a). The inclusions should remain warm so they can be evenly distributed throughout the nougat during kneading.

2 Prepare the nougat base: Blend the dried egg white with 1 ounce (30 g or 2 tablespoons) of the sugar and combine with the fresh egg whites in the bowl of a stand mixer fitted with the whip attachment.

3 Place the honey in a heavy-bottomed pot and heat to 248°F (120°C). When the temperature of the honey reaches 225°F (108°C), begin whipping the egg whites on medium speed.

4 When the honey reaches 248°F (120°C), pour it slowly into the egg whites (b), continuing to whip.

5 Meanwhile, combine the remaining sugar, glucose, water, and vanilla bean scrapings in a separate heavy-bottomed pot and heat to 311°F (155°C).

6 Add the rose water to the sugar syrup and pour slowly into the egg whites as you continue to whip, taking care to avoid getting syrup on the whip or on the sides of the bowl.

7 Increase the mixing speed to high, and whip for 3 minutes.

8 Add the melted cocoa butter and blend thoroughly (c). Warm the exterior of the mixing bowl with a kitchen torch, if necessary, to prevent any lumping of the cocoa butter (d).

9 Dust a flat work surface with confectioners' sugar. Remove the nougat from the mixing bowl, placing it on the sugared work surface, and gently add the warmed inclusions (e).

10 Fold and knead the mass until the inclusions are well distributed (f).

11 Place the nougat between two nonstick baking mats. With a rolling pin, roll the nougat into a 9 x 12-inch (23 x 30 cm) rectangle (g).

12 Let the nougat cool at room temperature. When cool, cut into desired shapes (h).

13 The cut pieces may be dipped in tempered couverture (i).

a   Combine the inclusions prior to warming.

b   Add the honey to whipped egg whites.

e   Add the warmed inclusions.

f   Fold in the inclusions.

c Add the melted cocoa butter.

d The finished nougat mixture.

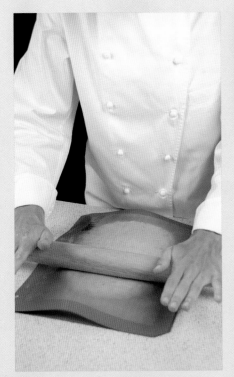

g Roll the nougat between nonstick mats.

h Cut the nougat.

i Optional: Dip the nougat into the tempered chocolate.

WHEN HE WAS A TEENAGER, WILLIAM LEAMAN HAD A PLAN, AND BY THE TIME HE WAS EIGHTEEN YEARS OLD HE WAS A PARTNER IN A BAKERY IN ARKANSAS. HE OBTAINED A GED, GETTING HIS FORMAL EDUCATION ON THE JOB IN BAKERIES. ATTRACTED BY THE VIBRANT FOOD SCENE AND LIFESTYLE OF THE NORTHWESTERN UNITED STATES, HE RELOCATED TO SEATTLE.

WILLIAM LEAMAN,
WORLD CHAMPION BAKER AND OWNER OF BAKERY NOUVEAU IN SEATTLE

A major step in his education came during his formal apprenticeship at the short-lived National Baking Center in Minneapolis. After completing his internship, he returned to Seattle to work for a large artisan baking company as the pastry chef. There, he developed new lines of high-quality chocolate candies, pastries, *Viennoiseries*, petit fours, and *entremets*. Yearning for more, he moved to Las Vegas to work as the pastry sous chef at the Paris Hotel under the tutelage of MOF Jean Claude Canestrier, continuing his education in the operation of a large, world-class pastry kitchen.

In 2005, William was the artistic design member of Baking Team USA at the *Coupe du Monde le la Boulangerie*. The team won the gold medal, and he was immediately on his way to training as the degustation member of a team at the National Pastry Team Championship, where he won the bronze medal.

His Bakery Nouveau, a full-line bread and pastry shop, has received every local and regional award available to retail bakers.

"Don't make what others want, make what you like and are passionate about—it's the only way to be authentic, remain enthusiastic, and continue to evolve in your craft."

INTERVIEW WITH WILLIAM LEAMAN

OTHER THAN BUTTER, FLOUR, SUGAR, EGGS, AND SALT, WHAT ARE THE FIRST TEN INGREDIENTS YOU WOULD SELECT FOR YOUR KITCHEN?

Chocolate, vanilla, Type 85 flour, various cheeses, fresh nutmeg, balsamic vinegar, good olive oil, fresh herbs, madras curry, and good wine.

OTHER THAN AN OVEN, WHICH ITEMS ARE ESSENTIAL TO EQUIP YOUR HOME KITCHEN?

A microplane grater, a wine key, a timer, a wheel or pizza cutter (useful for cutting all sorts of dough, pasta, etc.), and a well-cared-for 8-inch (20 cm) vegetable knife.

HOW HAS TECHNOLOGY CHANGED PASTRY MAKING?

Well, just in the last ten years, I think that pastry has developed faster than in the previous thirty, largely due to silicone. So many applications have been developed using it, from baking, to frozen items, to chocolate work, it just opened up a lot more options.

The techniques and tools used for such things as molecular gastronomy have opened up a lot of options in terms of flavors and textures, and many of these will eventually trickle down into more regular production.

YOUR PRODUCT SELECTION IS CONSTANTLY ROTATING AND EVOLVING, PROBABLY MORE THAN MOST BAKERIES. HOW DO YOU DEVELOP AND INTRODUCE NEW PRODUCTS?

I read constantly and look for ideas, techniques, or ways to change and update our product and flavor profiles. We are also lucky that the Seattle area is home to such a large and diverse amount of fresh fruit and produce. As we developed relationships with our vendors, we were able to get access to more seasonal items, and this lets me (and my staff) get more creative.

Development usually takes place by a process of thought, then a very brief trial period to work out the best display or portion size, or balance of flavors, and then we try out new pieces on a weekend or weekday and see how they do. Some items we keep for a while, some not very long. Sometimes we make something just because our vendor found some phenomenal local berries,

Also, there has been such an influx of new ingredients, and I think that the Internet as a technology really drove a rapid increase in the joys of fine pastry. It's also allowed for interactions and collaborations that beforehand might have been a lot more difficult, further driving the industry.

WHAT WAS THE MOST DIFFICULT SKILL FOR YOU TO LEARN WHEN YOU WERE BEGINNING?

I'd have to say working with chocolate. At the time, there weren't really that many resources—the artisan chocolate and confection movement hadn't really even started. You know, it was easy to work with in some things, like baking, but in terms of fine work, finished desserts, confections, and such, it was almost all experiential learning. Now we have a greater understanding of what's going on at the molecular level, and more of the whys and hows, which has led to better products. And the basics, at least, are easier to learn now, too.

WHAT IS YOUR THOUGHT PROCESS WHEN WRITING A PASTRY MENU?

It starts with considering the season and its ingredients. Some seasons are really short, like for apricots (two to three weeks), and after figuring out what I want to make, I have to plan and maximize how much we can do, whether it's one product or several, and then keep track of which are doing well and focus on those. We also consider colors—how will the case look? Our case is our visual menu, so we consider things like how balanced the colors are and if they show the season and indicate the possible flavors.

WHAT IS THE FIRST THING YOU TELL A NEW STUDENT?

Organization and a willingness to continually strive to work faster and more efficiently are two of the most important keys to being successful. That, and realize that there is always—*always*—something you can be working to improve, no matter what level you are at.

Also, don't bring your personal life to work. When you're here, you're working, leave the rest at the door and focus on the food. Anticipate, and don't be afraid to ask questions—there aren't any stupid questions (well, the same question over and over can be problematic in another way), but there are a lot of stupid assumptions, which can end up costing the shop money.

WHAT IS ONE UNIQUE GUIDING PRINCIPLE RULE OF YOUR KITCHEN?

I always encourage people to read professional journals, books, articles, and anything food related they are interested in. We have an extensive collection of books at the shop, and I encourage people to use them.

WHAT WOULD YOUR FANTASY PASTRY VACATION BE?

I'd love to spend time in Vienna. Working at Demel would just be amazing—getting immersed in that culture and food, and seeing the places where so much of what we know as pastry originated. There'd be so much to see and learn.

IF YOU WERE FORCED TO CHOOSE BETWEEN EATING BAKED GOODS OR MAKING THEM FOR THE REST OF YOUR LIFE, WHICH WOULD IT BE?

Eating, hands down.

HOW DO YOU STAY MOTIVATED?

Just keeping up with the business is enough to keep going. That, and there's just so much good food and produce in this area to experiment and play with.

YOU'RE PACKING A PICNIC WITH PRODUCTS FROM BAKERY NOUVEAU. WHAT'S IN YOUR BASKET?

A baguette and some good cheese, probably coffee (iced, double shot Americano), and then I'd steal my wife from the bakery office and run away.

WORDS TO LIVE BY?

Organize and make lists. Remember: It's food. It's about eating and living well and finding that balance. Don't make what others want, make what you like and are passionate about—it's the only way to be authentic, remain enthusiastic, and continue to evolve in your craft.

Yield: 40 sandwiched macarons

Prep time: active time, 1 hour; total time, 3 hours

Equipment needed: Food processor (optional), medium mixing bowl, stand mixer fitted with the whip attachment, small saucepan, piping bag fitted with medium plain (round) tip, 2 half sheet pans, 2 silicone baking mats

VANILLA BEAN MACARONS WITH MILK CHOCOLATE GANACHE
BY WILLIAM LEAMAN

Macarons have become the darling of pastry aficionados—and for good reason. The chewy shells are an excellent vehicle for carrying the flavors and textures of sweet and savory fillings. With a little practice, they are quite simple to produce. This is one of the few pastries that is made in a variety of colors. Displays of different colored macarons brighten any pastry presentation.

INGREDIENTS

	U.S. Imperial Weight	Metric Weight	Volume
Almond flour	10.6 oz	300 g	3 cups minus 1 tablespoon + 1 teaspoon
Confectioners' sugar	10.6 oz	300 g	2½ cups + 1 tablespoon + ¾ teaspoon
Vanilla bean			3 beans
Egg white			7 egg whites
Granulated sugar	10.6 oz	300 g	1⅓ cup
Water			⅓ cup + 1 tablespoon
Chocolate ganache (see page 145)			1 recipe

PROCEDURE

1 Combine the almond flour and confectioners' sugar. Sift together (a). Add the scrapings of the vanilla beans. (Alternatively, for a smoother macaroon, you may grind the almond flour, confectioners' sugar, and vanilla bean scrapings in a food processor fitted with the blade attachment and then sift.)

2 Mix three egg whites with the sifted flour mixture to form a smooth paste.

3 Place the remaining three egg whites in the bowl of a stand mixer fitted with the whip attachment. Begin whipping slowly. The egg white should be frothy at this stage.

4 Meanwhile, place the granulated sugar and water in a heavy-bottomed pot and cook to a temperature of 246°F (119°C), brushing the sides of the pot with a wet brush to prevent sugar crystallization (c).

5 Continue whipping the egg white on low speed while slowly adding the cooked syrup, being careful to avoid getting syrup on the sides of the bowl and the whip (d).

6 After all of the syrup has been incorporated, increase the mixing speed to medium high and whip until the sides of the bowl are cool to the touch. The meringue will be glossy, firm, and form a medium peak.

7 Fold one-third of the meringue into the flour/sugar paste. Incorporate thoroughly. Fold in another third of the meringue and incorporate thoroughly. Fold in the final third of the meringue (e).

8 Continue folding until the mixture is homogenous, soft, shiny, and flows evenly off the spatula (f).

9 Using a spatula, deposit the batter in a pastry bag fitted with a medium plain (round) tip. Twist the open end of the bag tightly to seal.

10 Using even, medium-firm pressure, pipe 2-inch (5 cm) rounds onto silicone baking mats (g).

11 Set aside at room temperature until the surface dries, approximately 30 to 60 minutes

12 Preheat oven to 200°F (93°C or just below gas mark ½).

13 Bake approximately 11 to 12 minutes. The surface of the macarons should be firm and dry, and the macarons will have "feet" (h).

14 Cool completely before removing from the baking mats.

15 Invert half of the macarons.

16 Make a slight depression in the center of the inverted macarons with your thumb to allow for more filling (i).

17 Pipe the softened milk chocolate ganache onto the inverted macarons (j). The ganache should be soft enough to spread to, but not over, the edge.

18 Place the remaining macarons on top of the ganache and gently press to adhere (k).

a Sift the almond flour and confectioners' sugar.

d Slowly pour the syrup into the whipped egg whites.

b Note the consistency of the batter after adding the egg white.

c Brush down the sides of the pot with a wet pastry brush while cooking the sugar syrup.

e Fold one-third of the meringue into the flour/sugar paste.

f Note the consistency of the final batter.

(continued)

g Pipe 2-inch (5 cm) rounds onto baking mats.

h The baked macarons.

i Use your thumb to make an indentation in half of the macarons.

j Pipe ganache into the indentations.

k Place the tops on the macarons and press to adhere.

Any flavor may be used in the macarons, and frequently, coloring is added to suggest the flavor. The use of coloring should be tasteful and sensible. The fillings may be varied to include additions to the ganache recipe, different ganaches, or buttercream.

Allowing the surface of the macarons to dry after piping them is a critical step. The mixture dries slightly, helping to retain the shape and create the "feet" on the bottom edge.

LAURENT BRANLARD, THE ONLY PERSON TO WIN THE WORLD PASTRY TEAM CHAMPIONSHIP TWICE, IS THE EXECUTIVE PASTRY CHEF AT THE SWAN AND DOLPHIN RESORTS AT DISNEY WORLD IN ORLANDO, FLORIDA. THE HOTEL HAS SEVENTEEN DINING OUTLETS AND MULTIPLE CATERING VENUES. LAURENT OVERSEES THE BAKING AND PASTRY NEEDS OF THE ENTIRE PROPERTY.

LAURENT BRANLARD,
RESTAURATEUR AND EXECUTIVE PASTRY CHEF AT THE SWAN AND DOLPHIN RESORTS AT DISNEY WORLD

He began his studies at the age of sixteen with an apprenticeship in France. He continued his studies until he had received certification as a pastry chef, a chocolate master, an ice cream maker, and a confectioner. He was a highly sought-after candidate for positions in some of France's top catering and restaurant operations before venturing to the United States and the U.S. Virgin Islands as a pastry chef for the Ritz-Carlton hotel company.

His chocolate and sugar showpieces have won numerous awards. He is known for intense focus, attention to detail, hard work, and exacting measures. He spends long hours in rigorous training for competitions, and he takes a similar approach to his job. In 2010, Laurent opened his first restaurant, LB Bistro and Patisserie, in the Sheraton Hotel & Towers in Chicago.

INTERVIEW WITH LAURENT BRANLARD

WHY DID YOU DECIDE TO BECOME A PASTRY CHEF?

It was just a kid's dream. My uncle had a restaurant, and with each visit to the kitchen, I knew I was getting inspired to become a pastry chef. The aromas, the sense of urgency, the attention to detail—it was intoxicating.

WERE YOU EVER UNDER THE TUTELAGE OF A MENTOR?

Not really. In my career, I have met a lot of very interesting and completely different individuals who taught me so many different things. I took the best from each, and eventually my own style and sense of taste emerged. The camaraderie and sharing among pastry chefs creates an atmosphere where everything is shared.

YOU ARE RECOGNIZED AS A WORLD LEADER IN CHOCOLATE WORK, SUGAR WORK, AND FINE PASTRIES. WHICH DISCIPLINE DO YOU MOST ENJOY?

Well, thank you for the compliment, but I think there are others who would qualify more than me in those categories. I try to do my best in every discipline that we have in our profession. It would be difficult for me to say that I like one more than the others. If you were to ask me to do a showpiece, I would probably do it in sugar since I think sugar is faster for me. I can get more impressive results in less time than I do with chocolate. But my all-time favorite category would be making pastries for a pastry shop.

WITH ALL THE DIFFERENT SKILLS AND INFLUENCES YOU HAVE, HOW WOULD YOU DEFINE YOUR STYLE?

I think it may be "elegant rustic," as this is what I like. When making pastries, I like to do traditional, well-executed recipes presented in an elegant way.

HOW DOES MANAGEMENT IN THE PASTRY KITCHEN DIFFER FROM MANAGEMENT IN THE BOARDROOM?

I think every manager adapts to his individual field, creating his own style for each situation.

WHAT IS THE MOST SATISFYING PART OF YOUR JOB?

The accomplishments in any category. In this business, we have the opportunity to accomplish many things and see the results: it can be a dessert menu or a buffet, a showpiece, etc. Or it can be a human accomplishment, such as [being] a teacher or trainer, when you take individuals and help them become what they were dreaming to be.

HOW DO YOU REMAIN MOTIVATED? HOW DO YOU REMAIN CURRENT?

I think the motivation comes from the passion that I have for this business. I am always looking at what other chefs are doing. Some are very creative and create the trends, so I watch, analyze, reproduce, and add my own touch, which sometimes takes me in another direction. I am just like any other pastry chef—we all look at each other and learn from each other. This is part of the evolution.

OTHER THAN BUTTER, FLOUR, SUGAR, EGGS, AND SALT, WHAT ARE THE FIRST TEN INGREDIENTS YOU WOULD SELECT FOR YOUR KITCHEN?

Chocolates, vanilla beans, heavy cream, fruits and fruit purées, nuts, nut pastes, glucose, gelatin, pectin, and yeast.

Opera rock!

OTHER THAN AN OVEN, WHICH ITEMS ARE ESSENTIAL TO EQUIP YOUR HOME KITCHEN?

A digital scale, saucepans, bowls, a whisk, spatulas, a rolling pin, a thermometer, and a stand mixer.

WHAT WAS THE MOST DIFFICULT SKILL FOR YOU TO LEARN WHEN YOU WERE BEGINNING?

Tempering chocolate. It requires a certain feel in addition to the scientific knowledge.

WHAT IS THE FIRST THING YOU TELL A NEW TEAM MEMBER OR STUDENT?

I say that the most important thing is to have a good spirit and a good attitude. I always say I can give you all my knowledge, recipes, and skills, but I cannot give you attitude, respect, and drive. Those have to come from you.

WHAT ARE THE GUIDING PRINCIPLES/RULES OF YOUR KITCHEN?

Respect—each other, yourself, the ingredients, the recipes, the equipment, and the customer.

WHAT DO YOU BAKE AT HOME?

Simple desserts, like crème brûlée. On Sundays, [I make] pizzas, tarts, brioche, and cookies.

WHAT WOULD YOUR FANTASY PASTRY VACATION BE?

Going to Asia, Japan in particular. I have never been there. Visiting cocoa planta-tions along the equator is another dream

WHAT IS YOUR GREATEST STRENGTH? WHAT IS YOUR BIGGEST WEAKNESS?

My greatest strength is determination. Listening is my weakness.

WORDS TO LIVE BY?

Perfect execution, passion, loyalty, honesty, and perseverance.

"I can give you all my knowledge, recipes, and skills, but I cannot give you attitude, respect, and drive. Those have to come from you."

DACQUOISE AU CHOCOLAT
BY LAURENT BRANLARD

Dacquoise au chocolat is a study in contrasts. It has a simple, understated appearance: one disc, dusted with powdered sugar, floating on a layer of creamy chocolate filling above a second disc. A crisp texture turns chewy as it melds with the smooth chocolate. Large versions are sliced in wedges, like a cake or tart. Individual units may be picked up by hand.

INGREDIENTS

	U.S. Imperial Weight	Metric Weight	Volume
Almond flour	2.8 oz	80 g	
Confectioners' sugar	2.8 oz	80 g	
Egg white			3 egg whites
Granulated sugar	1.1 oz	30 g	
Chocolate Mousse (see page 89)			1 recipe
Chocolate Ganache (see page 145)			1 recipe
Crème Chantilly (see page 17)			1 recipe

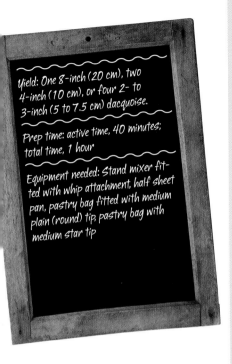

PROCEDURE (see photos, pages 170–171)

1 Preheat oven to 390°F (199°C or gas mark 6).

2 Draw two 8-inch (20 cm) circles on a sheet of baking parchment. Invert the parchment and place on a flat sheet pan.

3 Sift together the almond flour and confectioners' sugar (a). Reserve.

4 In the bowl of a stand mixer fitted with the whip attachment, whip the egg whites on medium speed.

5 When the egg white is frothy and foamy, add the sugar slowly while continuing to mix on medium speed.

6 Whip to a soft peak. The meringue should be glossy and firm.

7 Fold in the sifted flour–sugar mixture (b). Fold quickly and efficiently to prevent deflating the foam (c).

8 Using a spatula, place the mixture in a pastry bag fitted with a medium plain (round) tip.

9 On the inverted parchment in the sheet pan, pipe the batter to fill in the drawn circles, beginning on the outside edge (d).

10 Bake until the discs are golden and the edges are firm, approximately 15 minutes. Finish baking with the oven door slightly open for 1 or 2 minutes to dry out the discs. (The discs should be quite dry because they will contain a moist filling.)

11 Let cool, then remove the discs from the baking pan and trim the edges with a paring knife if they are too dark and/or dry.

12 Place one of the discs on a serving tray and pipe chocolate mousse (page 89) or whipped milk chocolate ganache (page 145) around the edge in a decorative pattern (e). Pipe crème Chantilly or chocolate mousse into the center (f).

13 Place a disc on top of the filling (g) and dust with confectioners' sugar (h).

14 Decorate with a rosette of the reserved filling. Garnish as desired (i).

15 Store and serve at room temperature. This pastry is best served the day it is made.

Why use granulated and confectioners' sugars in the same product? Granulated sugar helps set the protein matrix in the meringue that will provide structure in the final product. Confectioners' sugar is 3 percent cornstarch, which acts to dry and toughen, as well as provide structure.

Dacquoise discs may be piped and frozen for up to five weeks. Thaw, unwrapped, at room temperature. Fill as directed above.

a Sift the almond flour and confectioners' sugar.

b Fold the flour–sugar mixture into the meringue.

e Pipe chocolate mousse or whipped ganache around the baked edge.

f Fill in the center with crème Chantilly or chocolate mousse.

c Note the consistency of the finished batter.

d Pipe circles of batter onto prepared parchment.

g Place the second disc on top of the filling.

h Sift confectioners' sugar over the top of the *dacquoise*.

i Pipe a rosette of reserved filling in the center.

RESOURCES

TOOLS AND EQUIPMENT

ONLINE SOURCES FOR INGREDIENTS AND SMALL WARES

www.bakedeco.com
Quality supplies, tools, and equipment

www.bridgekitchenware.com
A wide variety of cookware and accessories

www.chefrubber.com
Colorants, transfer sheets, tools, and equipment

www.chefsresource.com
Tools, gadgets, cookware, and small appliances

www.fantes.com
Dependable source for cooks' wares since 1906

www.jbprince.com
Baking mats, bags, pastry cutters, tools, and more

www.le-sanctuaire.com
Herbs, spices, books, and small electrics

www.oldwillknotscales.com
Scales for every professional

www.pastrychef.com
Professional-grade tools and high-quality ingredients

www.pastryitems.com
Pastry cutters, baking mats, baking sheets, scales, and appliances

LITERATURE

www.chipsbooks.com

www.jessicasbiscuit.com

www.kitchenartsandletters.com

www.quarrybooks.com

EDUCATION

SCHOOLS OFFERING CONCENTRATED COURSES FOR SERIOUS PASTRY COOKS

At-Sunrice Global Chef Academy, Singapore
Professional training and weekend classes for enthusiasts
www.at-sunrice.com

CAST Alimenti, La Scuola Cucina, Brescia, Italy
Italian culinary school for professionals and serious cooks
www.castalimenti.it

The French Pastry School, Chicago, Illinois
World-class pastry chef instructors for professional and dedicated home cooks
www.frenchpastryschool.com

International Baking Academy, Weinheim, Germany
German Bread and Pastry Program
www.akademie-weinheim.de/international-academy.html

Johnson & Wales University, Providence, Rhode Island; Denver, Colorado; Miami, Florida; Charlotte, North Carolina
Associates and Bachelor's Degrees available, continuing education, and Chef's Choice classes for weekend warriors
www.jwu.edu

The King Arthur Flour Education, Norwich, Vermont
An ever expanding and rotating selection of classes for baking aficionados
www.kingarthurflour.com/baking/

The Lenotre Culinary and Pastry School, Plaisir, France
Professional training and advanced classes
www.lenotre.fr/en/ecoles_lenotre.php

The Notter School, Orlando, Florida
Professional programs for professionals and serious home bakers overseen by world champion Ewald Notter
www.notterschool.com

Richemont Fachshule, Lucerne, Switzerland
Professional and advanced training programs
http://richemont.zynex.ch/en/05_agb/content.htm

San Francisco Baking Institute, So. San Francisco, California
Professional and weekend baking programs
www.sfbi.com

Savour Chocolate and Patisserie School, Brunswick, VIC, Australia
Internationally trained award-winning chefs give instruction in making modern and exquisite chocolates and pastries
www.savourschool.com.au

PERIODICALS

café–sweets
Japanese pastry magazine
www.amazon.co.jp

Dessert Professional
www.dessertprofessional.com

Le Journal du Patissier
www.journaldupatissier.fr

Pastry and Baking North America; Pastry and Baking Asia Pacific
www.pastryna.com

Paticceria Internazionale
www.pasticceriainternazionale.it

So Good ...
www.sogoodmagazine.com

CONTRIBUTORS

Kanjiro Mochizuki
Japan

Frederic Deshayes
France

Iginio Massari
Italy
www.iginio-massari.com/en

Sebastien Rouxel
France

En-Ming Hsu
USA

Franz Ziegler
Switzerland
www.franzziegler.ch

Thaddeus DuBois
USA

Kirsten Tibballs
Australia
www.savourschool.com.au

Robert Ellinger
USA

Jordi Puigvert Colomer
Spain
www.sweetngo.com/skin/portal.aspx

Thomas Haas
Germany
www.thomashaas.com

Kim Park
(Kim, Deok-Kyu)
South Korea

Anil Rohira
India

Ewald Notter
Switzerland
www.notterschool.com

Lauren V. Haas
USA

William Leaman
USA
www.bakerynouveau.com

Laurent Branlard
France
www.sheratonchicago.com/lb/pdfs/laurent_branlard_bio.pdf

PHOTOGRAPHER CREDITS

Courtesy of Bakery Nouveau, 7 (bottom); 158
Kathrin Best, 122; 124
Courtesy of Laurent Branlard, 166; 167
Courtesy of Jordi Puigvert Colomer, 110; 112
Thomas J. Delle Donne, 137
Courtesy of Frederic Deshayes, 36; 39
Courtesy of Thaddeus DuBois, 84; 87
© Craig Ellenwood / Alamy, 31
© Brenton Ho, 62; 63; 64
Amos Morgan, 6; 7 (top)
Courtesy of Ewald Notter, 144
Gale Reeves, 157; 159
Courtesy of Sébastien Rouxel, 53; 55
Courtesy of Kirsten Tibballs, 92; 94; 95
John Uher Inc., 28; 45, 100; 102; 131
Courtesy of Franz Ziegler, 73; 74; 75

ABOUT THE AUTHOR

Nathan Mitchell Stamm is an associate instructor in the International Baking and Pastry Institute within the College of Culinary Arts at Johnson & Wales, Providence, Rhode Island. His area of specialization is artisan baking. He studied at Dunwoody Technical College in Minneapolis; the French Pastry School in Chicago; the San Francisco Baking Institute in San Francisco; and L'ecole Lenotre in Plasir, France.

In 2006, he won the silver medal and was recognized for best workmanship at the National Bread and Pastry Championship. In 2008, he won the award for artistic design at the National Bread and Pastry Championship.

His work has been featured in *Dessert Professional, Modern Baking, Rhode Island Monthly, Pastry's Best*, and *Pastry and Baking North America.* He is a consultant for bakeries and manufacturers as well.

Favorite color: bread
Ultimate goal: to be a Southern gentleman—it's a work in progress

ACKNOWLEDGMENTS

To all the previous generations who combined flour, butter, sugar, eggs, salt, and vanilla and transformed them into foods that give pleasure, joy, and historical context, I thank you for passing your knowledge to future generations.

I offer my thanks and appreciation to the faculty, administration, and staff of Johnson & Wales University. Thank you to Martha Crawford who hired me and encouraged me. Thank you to my baking brothers Ciril Hitz and Richard Miscovich for leading by example and bringing me along for the ride.

The pastry chefs who participated in this book reinforced my deep beliefs in the baking and pastry profession. Their contributions to the profession are well documented, but what is often overlooked is their warmth and generosity. They opened up their shops and their lives for this project so others can learn and grow. With travel and production demands greater than most of us can imagine, they met every deadline. This book would not exist without them. I salute you all; I will always be grateful.

To my family, the Speigels of Chicago, Illinois, the Stamms of Austin, Texas, and Aunt Miriam, thank you for your unwavering support. To the families who have adopted me throughout my baking and pastry travels, the Johnsons of Littleton, Colorado, and Gillettes of Hailey, Idaho, thank you for opening your homes and hearts to me. To the Hitz family of Rehoboth, Massachusetts, thank you for showing me the way and for mentoring me—with the book and in life.

To Didier Rosada, Philippe LeCorre, Matt MacDonald, and Kent Trebilcox: Thank you for teaching me that there is food in life and life in food.

To the students who donated their time, working selflessly behind the scenes, thank you for your patience, your efforts, and for inspiring me: Jesse McDonald, Christine Sylvester, Melissa Richards, Lauren Fedick, Alyssa Ringler, Lindsay Jacob, Kathleen Van Sicklin, and Allison Quinlan.

A special thank-you to pastry chef Tim Brown for assisting with the pastry production.

Thank you to Biagio Settepani and Ok-Kyung Choo for translating.

To the amazing people at Quayside Publishing Group, especially Rochelle Bourgault and Betsy Gammons, thank you for selecting me for this project and for kicking me in the pants when I needed it. I see that your dedication and professionalism is equal to that of the pastry chefs who were chosen for this project. Thank you to Julia Maranan for her seamless editing.

Kylee Hitz's photography of the process and the finished products transcend the products themselves. Thank you for your vision and your patience. Your photographs give life to the book.

Thanking everyone who has shown me kindness, generosity, second, and third chances over the years would require a separate book. I know that you know my sincere appreciation. Thank you everyone.

And a final thank you to the inventor of expandable waistline pants.